# CHILDREN'S TOYS and BOOKS

# CHILDREN'S TOYS and BOOKS

•

## Choosing the Best for All Ages from Infancy to Adolescence

•
•

**Doris McNeely Johnson**

•
•
•

CHARLES SCRIBNER'S SONS • NEW YORK

Drawings by Sandra Brashears Williams

Photographs not otherwise credited are by
Sandra Brashears Williams and Myles Johnson

Designed by Gene Siegel

Copyright © 1982 Doris McNeely Johnson

**Library of Congress Cataloging in Publication Data**

Johnson, Doris McNeely.
  Children's toys and books.

  Bibliography: p.
  Includes index.
  1. Toys.  2. Play.  3. Child development.
  4. Books and reading for children.   I. Title.
  GV1218.5.J63   1982   649'.5   82-10462
  ISBN 0-684-17767-6

Portions of this book appeared, in substantially different form, in The Creative Parenting Toy Guide © 1980 Doris McNeely Johnson.

This book published simultaneously in the United States of America and in Canada—
Copyright under the Berne Convention.

All rights reserved. No part of this book may be reproduced in any form without the permission of Charles Scribner's Sons.

   1 3 5 7 9 11 13 15 17 19  F/C  20 18 16 14 12 10 8 6 4 2

Printed in the United States of America.

The information given in this book is intended solely as a guide of broad general usefulness, and inclusion in this book does not constitute a guarantee of a product or its safety by the author or publisher.

*To my mom and dad,
who first helped me to explore the world of toys,
and to Myles Jr., Nia, and Anike,
three good reasons for my returning to that delightful realm*

# Contents

|  | Preface and Acknowledgments | viii |
|---|---|---|
| 1. | The Importance of Play and Toys | 1 |
| 2. | A Place for Toys, and Toys in their Place | 11 |
| 3. | Toys and Play in Infancy | 14 |
| 4. | The Childhood Years: Development and Diversity | 31 |
| 5. | Best-Loved Toys: Dolls and Stuffed Animals | 60 |
| 6. | The Miniature World of Dollhouses | 74 |
| 7. | Puzzles and Games | 83 |
| 8. | Children's Books | 105 |
| 9. | Toys for Children with Special Needs | 133 |
| 10. | Homemade Playthings | 159 |
| 11. | Toys and Television Advertising | 166 |
| 12. | Toy Safety | 172 |
|  | Bibliography | 185 |
|  | Directory of Sources and Manufacturers | 187 |
|  | Index | 193 |

# Preface and Acknowledgments

This book grew out of my own frustrating attempts twelve years ago to wade through the multitude of children's toys and find those I wanted for my child. At home with a new baby and just having graduated from college, I began to dig deeper into the history and importance of play and toys. I passed on the fascinating information I found in bits and pieces to other interested parents. I then began conducting interviews with parents to get a feel for what they did about buying toys and books for their children. Many people I talked to asked what items I would suggest they buy in various situations. It was such an important concern—yet there seemed to be no single comprehensive source of information. This book, then, was written to help fill that gap, and I hope it will prove useful to parents and to everyone involved in child care.

The many lists of recommended toys and books included here should not be considered exhaustive or definitive. There are sure to be items in every category that could be added. *Children's Toys and Books* is meant to be a starting point; it will familiarize you with what is available and provide guidelines to help you make the right choices for your child at every stage of his development.*

---

* The masculine pronoun has been used throughout the book only for the reader's convenience; it in no way indicates a disregard for female children. After all, I have two daughters in addition to a son!

If you have experiences with children's toys and books that you would like to share with me, I would be very happy to hear them. Please address them to me at P.O. Box 55258, Fort Washington, Maryland 20744.

Of the many people who assisted in the completion of this book, I would like first to give thanks and appreciation to my husband, Myles, who remained patient, encouraging, and helpful during the three years it took to write it.

I am indebted to Dr. Leon E. Wright, professor emeritus of Howard University, a special mentor who has taught me so much.

Elaine Shalowitz read the manuscript and offered many helpful suggestions, and Brenda Watson and Dee Mebane did the typing and always encouraged me in the project.

Burma and Brynda Whitted of the Child Life Department of the Howard University Hospital Pediatric Unit, and Jill Hall of the Association for the Care of Children in Hospitals, in Washington, D.C., gave me advice for the chapter on children with special needs; and Dr. Julian Perry commented on the toy safety chapter. Thanks also go to the staff of the F. A. O. Schwarz toy store, Georgetown Park, Washington, D.C., who graciously lent many of the toys illustrated, and to the Toy Manufacturers of America, who provided additional photographs.

Finally, I would like to acknowledge Bettie Hamilton, Janice Valentine, Sandra Isler, Esther McNeely, Virginia Usher, and the many other mothers and fathers who let me question them endlessly about their own experiences with children and toys. And to their children, I express gratitude and special affection.

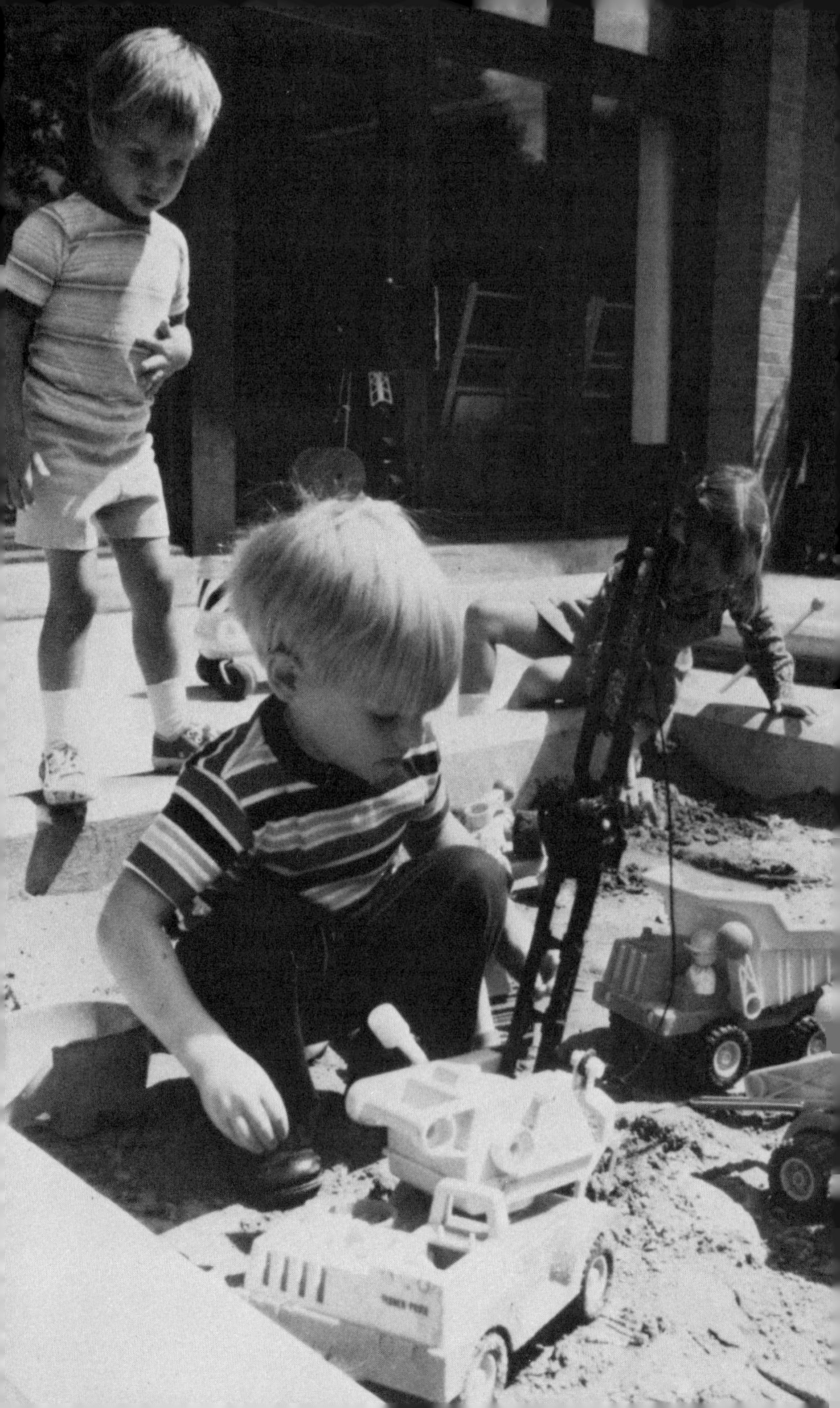

# 1
# The Importance of Play and Toys

What do we mean when we say that children play? Play has many definitions, but with regard to children, we can say that it is any activity that is engaged in freely, that is pleasurable, and that needs no reward beyond that which comes as a result of the activity itself. Children do not have to be told to play; they will do it for the sheer joy of it. It comes naturally, almost instinctively. And because of this, there is, on the part of some adults, a tendency to diminish its importance, to dismiss it as a simplistic and trivial activity of childhood. Nothing could be further from the truth; for play is inextricably intertwined with all aspects of children's development—physical, social, creative, and intellectual.

Play is children's work, and its importance cannot be overemphasized. For in playing, children are *doing*. They are active participants, not passive observers, in the joyous process of discovery and the organizing of information about their world. Research shows that the process of play begins in infancy as soon as babies are able to attend to events around them and have voluntary control over the parts of their bodies used in play.

This understanding of play is not new. Enlightened

(*Opposite*)
Photo by Larry Mulvehill, courtesy Toy Manufacturers of America

thinkers such as Socrates and Plato in antiquity, John Comenius in the 1600s, Friedrich Froebel (the originator of the kindergarten, or "garden of children"), Milton Bradley, and William James in the 1800s, Thomas Dewey in the early 1900s, and, more recently, Jean Piaget all recognized the importance of early play and toys in the overall development of children. They, among others, advocated teaching the child by allowing much self-discovery, using his interests and developmental levels as starting points (we can enter the child's world, but he cannot enter ours because he is incapable of thinking like an adult), and creating tools to mesh with those developmental levels. Fortunately, some toy companies today are doing just that.

## Play in Infancy

One mother steadfastly insists that her 8-pound, 14½-ounce firstborn played an interaction "game" with her on the second day of his life. She made the same loud swallowing sound that he did when he was breast-feeding. He did it again and paused, as if waiting for her to repeat it. She did and they continued feeding and playing. A few days later, she made the sound twice in quick succession, and her baby repeated it twice. They would play the "game" at almost every feeding and kept it up for months.

When told that the experts would probably doubt that an infant a few days old was capable of that kind of interactionary play, she just smiled and said, "That's okay. They used to say emphatically that the infant could not see for the first few weeks of life. Now we know that it can see a few hours after birth. The experts can be wrong."

Leaving the debate of just how early an infant starts playing, we can safely say that play definitely does begin during infancy. Certainly by the time babies are a few months old, they engage in play activities such as consciously smiling and cooing, making a sound for someone else to mimic or a fake cough that they do over and over again, or laughing when they are held up in the air. The child's response is likely to make the other person continue the game longer than if he made no response at all. In this way, by playing, the infant is beginning to exercise some control over his world. He discovers that he can make things happen: by producing a sound, he can get another person to make a sound. This idea of cause and effect is an important building block in the development of self-confidence and self-competence later on.

As the child moves through infancy, the play becomes more complex and toys become more important components of play activities. Toys become things to be handled rather than objects to just watch and listen to (such as mobiles and music boxes), as the child did immediately after birth. Much of his play with toys during infancy is actually solitary play; he is essentially playing by himself even though others may be present. Solitary play persists to some degree throughout childhood and into adolescence in activities such as working puzzles, painting or drawing, making models, and so on. As the child nears the end of infancy, we might see examples of parallel play—two toddlers playing alongside, but not really with, each other. Each has his own toy and is playing independently. These little ones may speak alternately and in turn, but their conversations may not even be related. It is as if each child is carrying on his own monologue, while also giving the other a chance to speak.

## *Associative and Symbolic Play*

As the child leaves infancy and moves into childhood, he begins to engage in associative play. Children become enmeshed in play situations and there is real interaction between players. ("You can be the mother and I'll be the baby. I'll cry and you feed me.") A larger portion of the child's day is given over to play activities, and the play becomes more involved.

One of the important functions play serves during childhood is the fostering of intellectual development. The conversations necessary for real associative play help to develop communication skills. When the child is engaged in some intense activity such as solving a puzzle, his powers of concentration are being developed. Many times in play, children will learn skills that are directly transferable to schoolwork. What is equally important is that these skills have been gained painlessly. For, ideally, learning should be as much fun as play.

The complexity of children's play is influenced by their growing mental capabilities. As they move through early childhood (ages 2–6), their language and play activities show increasing evidence of symbolism, making something stand for something else ("These two chairs are the train"; "Let's get our feet up so those sharks can't bite us"). Symbolic play allows the child to experiment with various adult roles such as mother, father, doctor, or teacher. Symbolic games such as hide-and-seek, being chased by a monster, frightening and being frightened provide the child with active outlets for dealing with subconscious fears. They also allow the child to face and overcome—or at least in some way to express—in fantasy feelings about situations that he is not ready or able to face in life, thereby relieving some of his tension and anxiety.

Even though many parents do not like Halloween, with all of its candy treats, it is the apex of this kind of fantasy play. The child gets a chance to be anything he wants. He can act out any character his imagination can conjure up. This symbolic transformation allows him to exercise great control over his environment in a way that he is not able to do ordinarily. He can cause some of the most wonderful effects of all time (in his estimation, not necessarily that of the parents)—getting candy and other typically forbidden or restricted sweets just by knocking on doors and threatening "trick or treat." Fantasy or symbolic play speaks to the child's needs and development on many levels, conscious and subconscious, throughout childhood and into adolescence.

Play gives the child opportunities to explore, examine, experiment with, and learn about the world he is a part of in his own individual way. As he moves through early childhood, his powers of concentration become greater. He can sustain an interest in a particular play activity for a much longer period of time. The richness of play at this age, from 4 or 5 years onward, is directly influenced by the experiences the child has had. Trips to the grocery store, a department store, farm, zoo, post office, museum, and the like may provide the impetus and information necessary to incorporate the experiences into play activities. The use of props and the appropriate accessories help to attribute greater importance to play.

Costumes or specific articles of clothing become necessary accompaniments to play. Young children may put on mother's shoes, gowns, jewelry, and cologne; or they may get out dad's pipe, hat, and shoes. Role models in play perform the behaviors of real life as accurately as the child can possibly achieve them. As more detail is assimilated, the play rendition achieves greater realism and depth. For example, the 6-year-old "mother" may now pick up the dolly to be burped after a feeding.

## *Physical Development*

From the initial reflexive, uncoordinated grasping attempts of the infant, his subsequent discovery of his hands and the play activity that emerges from the wonderful knowledge that "I can control these things," to the competitive athletic pursuits of the adolescent, physical activity is of special importance to the child's development.

As the infant develops physically to the point where he can grasp and voluntarily manipulate objects, he should be given toys to handle directly. Each time he shakes a rattle or sticks his foot in a crib jungle gym and it makes a sound, he is made aware of his physical abilities.

During the second year of life, when infants are able to move on their own, much of their play is strenuous activity that calls for great vigor of the large muscles. Propelling themselves across the floor on a tyke tryke, running, moving blocks and constructing with them—all contribute to the infants' muscular development.

It is interesting that at first most block play is done for the pleasure of the physical task. The blocks are used to build a very temporary structure that may be joyously demolished as soon as it is built. A 3-year-old might say, "Listen to this good sound when I knock these blocks down. It sounds like thunder." By the time the child is 4 or 5, however, the block building becomes more realistic. The child may set out to build a specific structure with the appropriate entrances, exits, windows, and even inhabitants. He may even want to save the structure for a time. The physical activity has become secondary to the creation of the structure.

Developing the small muscles of the eyes, fingers, and thumbs is also important in early childhood. Toys and play activities such as working puzzles, cutting with scissors, gluing and pasting, painting, and looking at books all encourage and facilitate small-muscle development as well as eye-hand coordination. These activities are an excellent preparation for the small-muscle actions of reading and writing. When parents understand the developmental sequence and the beautiful way in which development interacts with and is aided by play activities and toys, they can easily help their children grow in all areas.

During childhood, there should be a balance of many kinds of playthings that encourage both large- and small-muscle development. In late childhood (ages 6–12), children begin to participate in sports activities. They also begin to evaluate their own behavior. It is no longer enough just to achieve the feat; it must be done well. Children who are able to perform adequately on a physical level are likely to feel good about themselves, and, of course, much practice helps their performance.

### *Social Skills*

Social development begins in infancy, when the child plays the first interactive games with parents, such as peekaboo, cooing, imitating behavior, and so on. As the child leaves infancy, he develops associative play with friends and we see the beginnings of real social behavior. At this time the child gets the experiences of sharing, taking turns, showing respect for others' toys, accepting responsibility for cleanup, and many other social skills.

These skills are enhanced by the cooperative play activity of games. As intellectual development increases, children participate in simple games, then more complex ones that call for developing a strategy to anticipate the opponents' plans and allow for the formulation of a counterattack. With this level of social interaction, rules assume great importance, and there is much concern about justice and fair play.

## *Rediscovering Your Own Childhood*

One of the most fascinating and delightful things about children and their toys is that they encourage adults to rediscover and reexplore their own childhoods. You can unselfconsciously participate in games and activities that you would feel silly playing if there were no children around. Just walking through a toy store and seeing things that you played with or remember from your childhood can evoke pleasant memories. It also gives you a baseline from which to help guide your own children in the formation of childhood memories.

We have to be careful not to overdo this interest in our children's activities to the point where we are trying to relive or make up for our own childhoods. Adults should not control or intrude into children's play by giving advice when it is not asked for, correcting and making suggestions concerning their artwork, directing their dramatic play, or adjusting their block creations. Telling the child that "You have to put the big blocks at the bottom or your house will fall" is an intrusion. The child will eventually discover this himself, and it is important that he be allowed to do so. It's another situation entirely, of course, if the child cries and complains that "These stupid blocks keep falling down." Then the parent can ask if he or she might help, explaining how it is done and how the child will be better able to do it himself the next time. If the child refuses help, however, the parent should be patient enough and secure enough not to interfere.

I've been delighted on numerous occasions when my mentioning the fact that I played with a particular toy has generated instant interest in a child. Sometimes, though, the indirect response of "Oh, how very boring" has been strongly communicated. When this happens, we must be sensitive to the needs and wishes of our children, swallow our enthusiasm, and move on.

Now, having been duly warned about being intrusive, but understanding the vital functions that play serves, both parents should spend some time playing with each of their children, preferably at the child's invitation. This gives play so much more importance to the child. Parents can "eat" the food their children prepare, acknowledge and sometimes "babysit" their dolls, read to them, play games with them, and so on. One father liked his son's block structures so much that he took pictures of them. Imagine how the boy felt—his block buildings were so great that his dad wanted to have a record of them.

In a film entitled *The Lively Art of Picture Books*, Maurice Sendak, the noted author and illustrator of children's books, was asked, "Why do you go to so much work just for children?" His answer was: "This work stems from an endless fascination with childhood, an absorption with childhood. Simply an obsession about my own childhood. An attempt to re-create something which was once so important to me, a constant finding in my work, something which I don't ever want to lose again. Something probably more important to me than anything else in my life, so that there is no question as to why I do it. I have to do it. It's a necessity. I want to do it for the rest of my life, I'm certain."

Perhaps we should all be obsessed to some degree by our own childhoods in order to sensitively enter our children's worlds. If we approach the choosing of toys and books for our children thoughtfully and with a wellspring of knowledge and experience, we will be less likely to fall victim to the practice of buying only heavily advertised, often not very durable, unsafe, limited-value products. This is not to say that our every toy purchase will be a resounding success, but at least we can significantly increase our odds. For our children, varied play activities and toys are not optional; they are an essential part of balanced growth and optimum development.

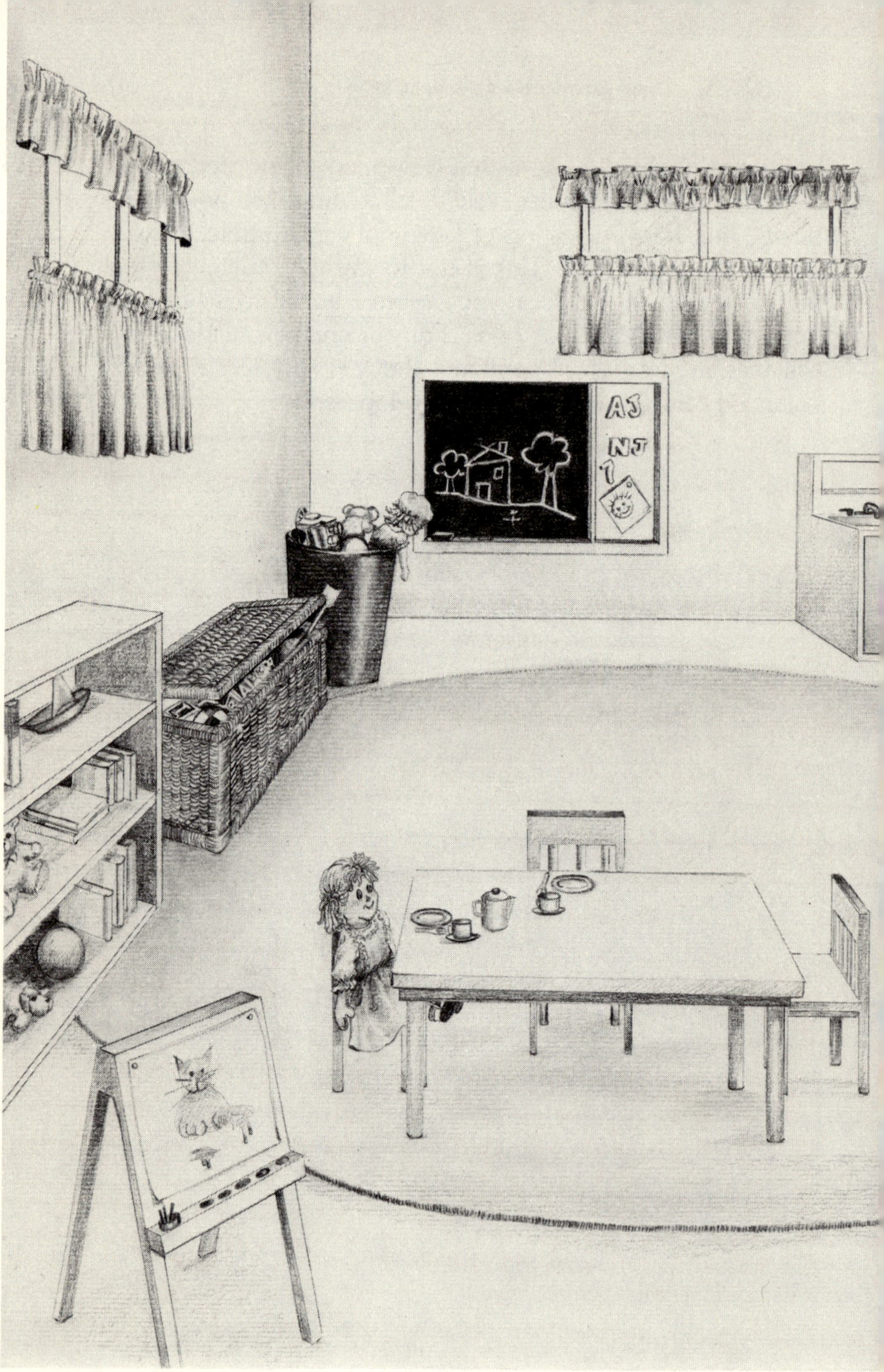
AJ
NJ

# 2
# A Place for Toys, and Toys in their Place

In every home there should be a special place set aside for toys and for children to play. In addition to providing a haven where children can enjoy their delicious clutter in total freedom, this reduces the chances that someone will fall over a toy. Have you ever noticed how children never seem to trip over their toys, it's only adults who do? You can bet that on the rare occasion when a child does fall over a stray toy, that is the perfect moment to talk—after comforting the child—about why it is so important to put toys back in their proper place.

How much space should be given over to toys? This depends, of course, on the number of children and the available area, but it should be as much room as you can spare. Some lucky children have a whole playroom set aside for their activities. If this is the case, you might put only the more action-oriented toys in the playroom. Items for quiet-time activities could be kept in the child's bedroom. These might include books, coloring books, records and record player, paper dolls, and workbooks. This way, after bathtime, the child could spend fifteen or twenty minutes in bed winding

(*Opposite*)
*Several different types of toy storage have been used in this play area, and the chalkboard/bulletin board on the wall helps to further define it as the child's space.*

down for sleep, quietly listening to a story, looking at a book, or playing the record player softly. Sometimes the promise of a story or the chance to hear a new record will serve as an incentive to cooperate in the bathing and getting-into-pajamas procedures.

If, like most of us, you are unable to devote a whole room to toys, it is important that a corner or some special area be given over to them. In it hang a bulletin board or set aside some wall space on which to pin up your child's creative masterpieces. This wall display will help to stamp your child's own signature on the area. There should also be some form of storage for toys in the play area. This can vary from a complete wall system of shelves and cabinets to a simple toy box or an unfinished pine or plastic shelf. The point is to have some place for the toys to "belong" after play so that the child begins to develop some feeling of responsibility for putting them away when he is finished with them.

## *Toy Boxes*

In choosing a toy box, be sure that it is one without any kind of locking mechanism that might allow the child to crawl in, get accidentally locked in, and suffocate. Also beware of hinged tops that can pinch fingers. In my experience, rattan baskets make excellent toy chests; some of them have tops that can be completely removed so that the danger of pinched fingers is eliminated. There is no chance of the child getting locked in one of these, and they are inexpensive, sturdy, and long-lasting (one of ours has been in use for eight years), and additional ones can be purchased as they are needed.

Another excellent candidate for a toy box is the large, brightly colored plastic container that looks like a small trash can and is typically used to store kitchen items. It has a top, but the metal fasteners that keep the top tightly sealed can be removed. These sturdy containers are more expensive than the rattan baskets, but if you want the toy boxes covered and prefer the bright colors, they are ideal.

## *Cleaning Up*

Your own particular circumstances and general attitude about neatness will dictate how frequently toys must be put away. For example, if you are in an apartment and have given over a corner in the eating area to play activities, you might not be able to sit and enjoy your dinner staring at a disheveled heap of toys. So the rule might be that toys are put away every day before dinnertime. If your children have a playroom, the requirement might be to have a thorough cleanup once a week.

One of the major functions of the toy area is to help the child get a sense of order in his world through the practice of returning toys to their proper place. By age 2, the child should begin to do some of this picking up. Initially, the parents will have to do most of the work, but all the while they should be psychologically preparing the toddler to assume the responsibility. As you are putting away the toys, you might ask your child to "Bring me that doll so we can put it in the toy box." Even if he will not bring it at first, you can get it, saying, "We have to put our toys away so they won't get broken, lost, or make somebody fall." Thus, even though the child is not actually doing anything, he or she is at least *hearing* what ought to be done, and this will gradually take effect.

When your child understands what a promise is, you can get him to promise to put the toys away before you allow him to take them out. What you want to do is enlist the child's cooperation in a very necessary disciplining process, and not allow cleanup to become a hostile battle of wills.

# 3
# Toys and Play in Infancy

The first toys of infancy should be ones that stimulate the senses of sight and hearing, not necessarily ones that can be manipulated. Newborn infants do not have enough voluntary control over their muscles to handle a toy. At first, their muscular movements are reflexive, uncoordinated, and jerky. Therefore, even if you put a rattle into a baby's balled-up fist (babies reflexively keep their hands balled into fists the first few weeks after birth), he will more than likely hit himself in the head with it, cry from the pain, and never realize that he himself was the originator of the pain. When the infant is a few days old, a rattle is not a "toy." Rattles and hand-held toys should be given to the infant after a few months, when he is well aware of them and can reach for and grasp them voluntarily.

Even though infants are not capable of voluntary muscular reactions immediately after birth, recent research has shown that they can do much more than had been previously thought. In the late 1800s the psychologist William James supposed that the world must appear terribly chaotic, confusing, and disorganized to a newborn, who probably perceived it as "one great blooming, buzzing confusion." Now it is generally agreed that James and others who believed this were wrong. It seems that the newborn emerges from the womb into an

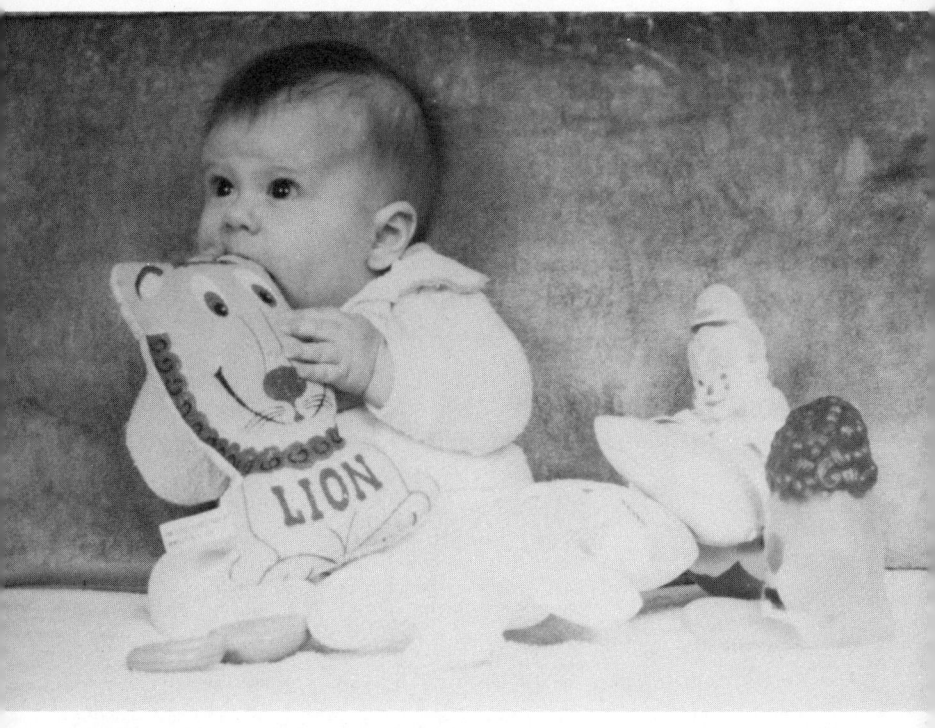

*Toys for infants should be "mouthable."* Photo by Larry Mulvehill, courtesy Toy Manufacturers of America

extensive, complex, and delicate web of conditions that mesh intricately and effectively with his preprogrammed capabilities and inborn skills, allowing him to immediately begin learning about and organizing his world. In other words, almost from birth (and maybe even before) the infant is learning about and interacting with his environment. All of his sensory apparatus is functioning, at least in some elementary way, from birth onward.

For example, the newborn infant can not only smell, but can distinguish between various odors. A sweet fragrance on a cotton swab held under his nose will not cause him to turn away, whereas an acrid smell will. There is also evidence that newborns quickly learn to distinguish their mothers' body smells from those of others. An interesting experiment demonstrating this was conducted at Oxford University. Two breast pads—one that had been worn by one infant's own breast-feeding mother, and a second that had been worn by another breast-feeding mother—were placed in the crib on each side of the infant's head. By the time he was 7 days old, he would spend significantly more time turned toward his own mother's breast pad than the other one.

The infant's hearing is also well developed and operating to a significant degree immediately after birth. In fact, there is even evidence that the fetus can hear before birth. The newborn seems to prefer sounds that are pitched about the same as the normal human voice rather than loud or shrill noises. He also appears to like and be soothed by rhythmic sounds such as a human heartbeat and the ticking of a clock or metronome.

At birth, a baby's sense of touch is well developed and functioning. He will attempt to withdraw from any painful stimulation, moving his foot, for example, if pricked by a sharp object. He seems to be soothed by being held and cuddled, and at first seems to derive some comfort from being wrapped snugly.

Babies are also born with taste discrimination ability. They can tell the difference between two liquids and will prove this by sucking one liquid and not another. The newborn will most readily accept sweetened liquids and reject salty or bitter ones.

Now we come to the fifth sense, that of vision. The advice given by past generations that the newborn infant cannot see and therefore must be kept in dim light for the first few weeks of life is apparently an old wives' tale. In the last ten to fifteen years, researchers have found that the newborn can indeed see a few hours after birth. Can he see as well as an adult? No, probably not, but there are certain visual feats that he is able to perform.

For example, he will turn his head from side to side to

follow a pinpoint of light in a dimmed room. When we look at something like a ball with both eyes, instead of seeing one ball on the right and one on the left, we merge the two images into one. Initially, a newborn probably sees two balls. But by the time he is about 4 weeks of age and has gained a measure of control over his eye muscles, he sees a single image. His vision is also different in that he is able to bring something into clear focus only if it is held about 7 to 15 inches from his eyes. It is as if his vision functions like a fixed-focus camera. Everything closer or farther away is blurred and out of focus. The newborn seems to want a moderate amount of visual stimulation and will seek it out. If you give him a choice between watching a plain white card or a card with a checkerboard design, he will tend to choose the checkerboard design to focus on longest. If he is given a choice between looking at an object that is stationary and one that is moving, he will choose the moving object.

It is as if the infant comes to us like a computer with some elementary programs already in place. This means that we can begin almost immediately to enlarge these "programs" by providing a stimulating environment.

The parent of an infant today is much luckier than those of past generations with regard to the choice of playthings. There is now a wide variety of excellent infant products and toys on the market, and the knowledgeable parent should have no problem making a selection.

## *The Sights of Infancy*

Change and stimulation are necessary, even in the crib. While lying on his back, the infant can see the ceiling of his room, the upper walls, and the sides of the crib—usually all white. On his stomach, he can see the crib sheets and the sides of the crib. We should immediately begin to ensure that this environment provides varied visual stimulation for the newborn infant.

Put up decals or figures on the ceiling. Some kind of temporary attachment would be best so that they can be changed from time to time. One enterprising nursery teacher put the names of all the children on the ceiling of the classroom. At naptime, you could see many of the children focusing on the brightly colored letters, tracing them with their fingers and quietly forming letters or names with their lips before dropping off to sleep.

A wallpaper border with animals or a colorful parade of children or other figures marching around the room can provide hours of interested gazing and fantasy creating. Pictures can also be placed on the walls, and when the infant can stand in his crib, he will be able to see decals placed anywhere on them, even at the bottom.

In the crib, we can use a bumper guard with figures or shapes decorating it, or we can use printed sheets (probably not both). We might also buy printed nightgowns and pajamas. One night after bathtime, I was putting my 1-year-old into a pair of Carter's pajamas with a printed top showing flop-eared dogs sitting by a bunch of flowers. It occurred to me that if I could see the dogs right-side up, when she looked at them they would be upside down. Then I saw that some of the dogs were right-side up and some were upside down; whoever was viewing them—the wearer or the spectator—would see some dogs in the correct posture. How smart of Carter's to plan for that!

Even the nursery floor can be made a source of varied and vivid visual stimulation. Brightly colored or variegated carpeting is a good choice. Also, an inexpensive floor covering with many different textures, colors, and shapes can be made by gluing and/or sewing carpet samples together. As the infant moves out of the crib and begins to explore his environment, he will get a variety of visual and tactile sensations from the carpeting. Both my daughters used this type of nursery rug to help learn their colors. Endlessly they played the game of stepping on a patch and saying, "What color is this, Mommy?" Another advantage of this type of rug is that if a piece gets badly soiled or damaged, it is very easy to take it up and replace it with a fresh one.

## *The Sounds of Infancy*

A toy that we can use early in infancy to provide auditory as well as visual stimulation is a crib mobile that contains a music box. Fisher-Price makes an excellent one, the Music Box Mobile, which has plastic farm animals and a farmer suspended from a thick nylon cord. I have seen some mobiles—which I do not recommend—that consist of brightly colored, rigid plastic birds. While these may be adequate for a very young infant, by the time the child is able to pull himself up and touch them, there is the danger of his breaking off and swallowing a piece as well as being cut by one of the sharp edges. There are also some mobiles with figures made of a soft, spongy material; with these it is possible that after the infant gets teeth (at around 5 months) and is able to pull himself up in the crib, he could bite off some of the pieces and swallow them. The cords of string that suspend the figures on the mobile should be of woven nylon or some other equally strong material so that the objects cannot be pulled off. Also, cords holding the objects onto the mobile should be short so that the infant cannot become entangled in them when he begins to pull himself up in his crib. (See chapter 12 for more about toy safety.)

Other toys that offer auditory stimulation, even before the infant has the muscular control needed to directly interact with them, are the Wagging Musicals stuffed toys made by Eden, which gently move their heads when wound up. A new and excellent toy is the Rock-A-Bye Bear by Rushton that makes sounds similar to those the infant heard in the womb before birth—the movement of the amniotic fluid and a heartbeat. These sounds tend to be soothing to the newborn. Other "toys" that are soothing are a ticking clock and a metronome. The infant should also be talked to constantly from the first day of birth. Research shows that infants who are denied auditory, visual, and tactile stimulation experience intellectual and social deficiencies they may never be able to overcome.

### *The Mouth as a Tool for Exploration*

We must not think of the infant's mouth solely in the way we do an adult's—as something for eating, communicating, and showing affection. For the infant, the mouth is also a tool to explore and get information about his environment. He is not necessarily trying to eat everything he puts in his mouth. Along with satisfying an innate need to suck, he is trying to learn something about the particular object, much as he does by using his eyes and ears. Because of this, infants will always put playthings into their mouths. It is important to give them chewable, "mouthable" toys—toys that can be sucked on without danger. We may see especially heavy chewing on toys during teething. The baby's toys should

- be too large to be swallowed
- be totally immersible in water and easily cleanable
- be colored with nontoxic lead-free paint (if paint is used)
- contain no small pieces

Some suitable toys for this stage of an infant's development are:

- Fisher-Price's crib and playpen puzzles, crib and playpen teethers and rattles, tub and pool toys, Snaplock Beads
- Playskool's Tub Pets, Happy Teethers, Bunny Ball, Baby's Doll
- Childcraft's Teething Jack
- Johnson & Johnson's Tracking Tube
- completely washable rag dolls, made by many manufacturers

## *Self-Awareness*

During the period of infancy (birth to 2 years), a multitude of important behavioral changes take place. Physically, the child moves from being a passive onlooker to becoming a self-locomoting, talking interactor with his environment. Socially, he moves from a totally self-centered, nonsocial being to one who becomes aware of others and is integrated into the family. Psychologically, he becomes aware of himself as a separate entity and also develops feelings, either positive or negative, about himself. Intellectually, he takes great strides in learning about, classifying, and putting some order into his world. And all of these far-reaching changes are taking place in a coordinated, interconnected fashion.

How do we choose toys that will pave the way for these crucial developmental changes? First, let's talk about two very important factors. The infant is beginning to form an idea of who he is; and to facilitate this self-awareness, he should be able to see himself. So, one important early-infancy toy is a nonbreakable mirror. Parents should also play with the infant in front of a large-scale mirror. Although she is not able to prove it scientifically, one mother reported that she was privileged to experience her firstborn's discovery of himself as a physical entity at the age of about 5½ months. He was being held in his mother's arms as she stood in front of a mirror. He looked into the mirror at both figures. He then gazed principally at the reflection of his mother. He looked from the mirror to his mother's face and back again with a characteristic frown on his face that typically meant he was thinking. Then he looked at his own reflection and there was an exuberant and excited jump, almost out of his mother's arms. His face broke out into a wide grin and pure joy poured from him in the form of a 5½-month-old's version of a yell. It was as if he worked out in his mind that "If this person next to me is the same one I see reflected in the mirror, then that other 'thing' I see next to her must be 'me'!"

As the infant is becoming self-aware, he is at the same

time developing feelings about himself, a concept of himself. Self-awareness says, "I am"; self-concept says, "This is the way I feel about what I am," and these feelings can be either positive or negative.

Unfortunately, or maybe fortunately, there are no toys that directly influence an infant's self-concept. The infant gets feelings about himself by the way others respond to him. If someone responds to his needs quickly and reliably, so that when he's hungry, he is fed and when he cries, he is comforted, then he will internalize the idea that the world (embodied in his mother, father, or primary caretaker) treats him well. He can, therefore, *trust* the world to meet his needs; he is treated this way because he is good. If he feels good about himself, then we say that the infant has a positive self-concept.

By the same process, if there is no one to immediately and predictably meet the infant's needs, he perceives that the world treats him badly because he is bad. He cannot trust the world to meet his needs. These feelings lead him to develop a negative self-concept. Some psychologists feel that the self-concept or the way a person feels about himself is at the very core of and influences his entire personality, even the way he interacts with the world of play and toys. So, at the very least, we want to start our babies off with a good feeling about themselves.

At this stage the infant is also introduced to the very important concept of cause and effect. For example, we may strap a crib gym to the side bars of the crib. When the infant sticks his hand or foot in one of the loops and shakes it, it makes a rhythmic sound. More important than the sound alone is the fact that the infant is getting a rudimentary lesson in cause and effect. He learns that *he* is the cause of the noise. Many psychologists feel that this is a very important concept for the child to begin to internalize. The child's seeing a connection between what he does and what happens in the environment is related to a personality characteristic labeled internal-external control. A person who is externally controlled sees no connection between what he does and what happens to him or his environment. Even if *good* things happen to him, but always outside of his control, it can lead to a feeling of externality. If a person feels that his behavior makes no difference, he will not develop self-confidence, self-competence, and initiative. He will become apathetic because he feels that no matter what he does, it makes no difference.

On the other hand, a person who is internally controlled is one who sees a connection between what he does and what happens to him. He sees a connection between his behavior and its effects. This helps him to develop self-confidence, self-competence, and initiative. He will be self-disciplined. He will take ultimate responsibility for his behavior and its effects.

Children need to be provided with toys that allow them to see some connection between their behavior (the cause) and what the toy does (the effect). The following are some examples of cause-and-effect toys that can start the movement to internality:

- teethers that make a sound when moved
- crib gym
- Jack-in-the-box
- squeeze toys that make a sound when pressed or chewed on (be certain to check that the squeaker is completely enclosed in the toy and cannot come apart and be swallowed)
- Kohner's Busy Box
- Playskool's Tote 'N' Play, Clik Clak Duck, Clik Clak Bunny, Baby Chimes, and Baby Flutter Ball
- Fisher-Price's Bath Activity Center, Activity Center, Happy Apple, Chime Ball, Push-Along Clown, Roly Raccoon, Melody Push Chime, Push-Along Rattle Ball, Xylo Drum, Jumping Jack Scarecrow, Funflower, Miss Muffett Play Pillow, Clik 'N' Clatter Car, Corn Popper
- Gabriel's Busy Box, Disney Musical Busy Box, Jolly Juggler, Busy Turtle, Busy Peek-A-Boo, Chiming Busy Roly Poly, Play Bells

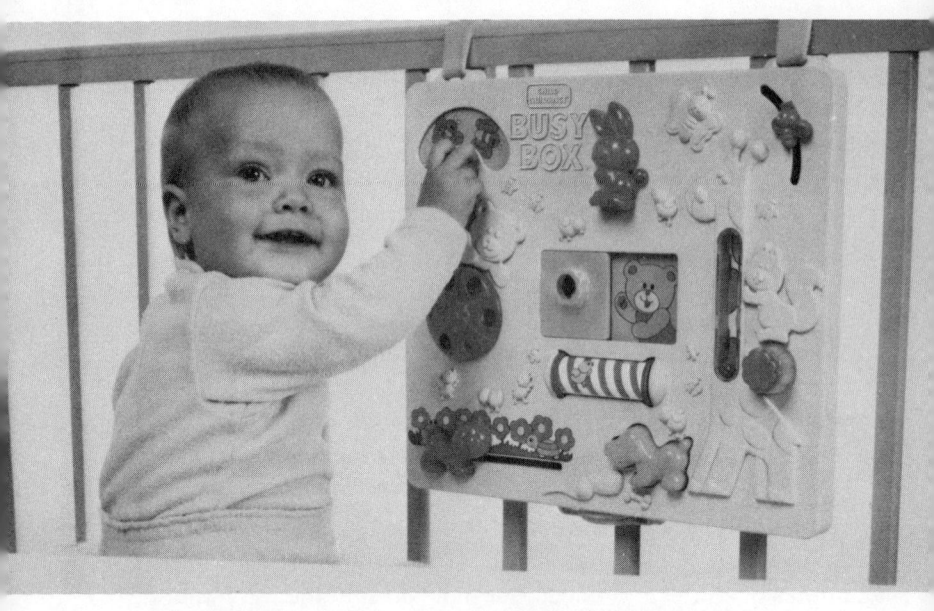

*Child Guidance's Busy Box.* Courtesy Child Guidance

- Child Guidance's Busy Box, Pound A Round
- Johnson & Johnson's Playpath playthings—Tracking Tube
- Childcraft's Pram Spinners Cradle Symphony, Action Stacks, Baby Trainer, Jack In The Crib

*Rattles*

As rattles are typically one of the first toys given to infants, special consideration should be exercised in choosing them. Rattles, it is felt by some, were not originally toys for infants but may have served some religious function. Researchers think that the first rattles were probably gourds or other fruits that dried, leaving their seeds free-floating on the inside. In some ancient cultures these rattles may have been used to frighten evil spirits away. No one knows how many thousands of years it took for the rattle to evolve into a toy for infants. Perhaps some busy cave mother noticed how her child stopped crying as she was ritually ridding the cave of hungry, unwelcome spirits before dinner.

Today, rattles are almost exclusively toys for the very young. As mentioned previously, the rattle and all other hand-held toys should not be introduced until the infant is reaching for things and grasping on his own. The rattle should be too big to be put in the infant's mouth and should be constructed of nonrigid plastic. (For additional safety considerations regarding rattles, see chapter 12.)

Suitable rattles for the infant include:

- Childcraft's Peek-And-See Rattle
- Fisher-Price's Look-At-Me-Elephant, Baby Butterfly, Hippo Wheel, Flower Rattle
- Johnson & Johnson's rattle

## *Physical Development*

By the time the infant is 1 year old, he is usually walking. The second year of infancy involves much physical activity and many toys facilitate the development of the large muscles, including push-and-pull and ride-on toys that allow the infant to propel himself from place to place. Some recommended push-and-pull toys are:

- Fisher-Price's Push-Along Clown, Roly Raccoon, Push Chime, Corn Popper, Melody Push Chime, Mini-Copter, Toot Toot Engine, Snoopy Sniffer, Queen Buzzy Bee, Bob-Along Bear, Tag-Along Turtle, Little Snoopy, Suzie Seal, Chatter Telephone
- Playskool's Letter Block Wagon
- Child Guidance's Happy Frog, Clutch Doggy, Play Train
- Hasbro's Digger The Dog

Ride-on toys, which allow the infant to propel himself by his own power, include:

- Childcraft's Rock 'N' Ride Lion, Creative Rider
- Fisher-Price's Little Red Riding Wagon, Riding Horse, Creative Coaster, Explorer
- Playskool's Big Yellow Toddler Taxi, Toddler Truck, Tyke Bike
- Empire's Tot-A-Bout Trike, Tot-A-Bout Car
- Wonder's Bucky The Horse, Scooter Frog, Walk-R-Ride
- Little Tikes' Tike Wagon, Ollie Coaster

## Intellectual Development

In addition to making great physical strides, the infant is also progressing by leaps and bounds intellectually. He is interacting with the environment and gaining a great deal of information from this interaction—by using his sensory experiences to provide data to fill in his rudimentary "computer programs." At this stage, much learning is a "hands-on" experience. Many infants enjoy experimenting with simple household items such as pots, pans, and wooden and plastic containers. Toys that help the child perceive shapes and corresponding spatial relationships—which block fits into which hole—include:

- Playskool's Postal Station Shape Sorter, Teddy Bear Shape Sorter, Play Phone
- Child Guidance's Learning Block
- Fisher-Price's Shape Sorter, Baby's First Blocks, Plastic Beads and Blocks
- Childcraft's My Mail Box

Nesting toys are groups of objects that are of graduated sizes and which fit into or stack onto each other to show the relationship of largest to smallest. For 2-year-olds, recommended toys of this kind include:

*Playing with Fisher-Price's Rock-A-Stack.* Photo by Larry Mulvehill, courtesy Toy Manufacturers of America

- Playskool's Stacking and Nesting Assortment of barrels, eggs
- Childcraft's Stacking Cones
- Fisher-Price's Rock-A-Stack
- Child Guidance's Stack Rings
- nesting cubes and, as the child gets greater manual dexterity, the Russian Matreshka (variant spellings: Metruska, Metriushka) or nesting dolls

Toys that can be fitted together and taken apart help the child to begin to understand the concept of reversibility, an important intellectual ability. He learns that he can start with the toy intact and take it apart; then, by reversing the steps, he can put it back together into one unified whole. The child must have many chances to experiment concretely with reversibility in a toy before he can later reverse a set of steps symbolically in his head. Toys that give experience with reversibility include:

- Ideal's Pull Aparts: Loco, Telephone, Teapot, Iron, Tea Kettle, Ring-A-Bell
- Playskool's Color Stacking Discs
- Duplo's Tugboat, Delivery Van, Sportscar, Pony Trailer
- Brio's Polly, Clown, Puck, Max Dachshund, Small Cat, Small Owl, Tommy, Freddy

Construction or building toys should also be included in the play activities of the toddler. Alphabet blocks allow him both to construct and to begin to develop familiarity with letters. Playskool's Number Wood Blocks have numerals on them rather than letters. Playskool also makes Bristle Blocks, Unit Blocks, and Table Blocks; Childcraft manufactures Unit Blocks; and Duplo offers Rock 'N' Rattle, Rattle And Roll. These building toys help develop eye-hand coordination, manual dexterity, and powers of concentration.

## Artistic Adventures

The infant, during the latter part of the second year, may also begin creative activities using crayons or magic markers on paper. Typically, the first markings will be linear, showing a great deal of back-and-forth movement. Even these seemingly random lines can yield something beautiful, if the child is given brightly colored crayons or magic markers with which to make them. These materials require some rather stringent overseeing at first to teach the child to mark only on the paper. However, I do not think there is one parent in the world who has escaped having at least one "on-the-wall" painting done by a budding artist. Be sure to buy the large primary-sized crayons, as a child of 2 does not have enough control in the small muscles of the fingers to manipulate the small crayons.

## Books in Infancy

Infancy is the time to introduce the child to the world of books. Two excellent types of first books are ones made of soft cloth and those made of very thick-paged cardboard.

The cloth books may remind us of our own childhoods, and every infant ought to have a couple purely for the sake of tradition. The thick-paged cardboard books are very sturdy and can take the banging and other rough treatment likely to be given them by the nonreading infant. These books typically have pictures of children engaged in various activities, objects of a particular color on each page, pictures of numerals and the corresponding number of objects, or large pictures of playthings typically used by infants such as a block, a rattle, or a ball. Parents may use these books to introduce the child to the process of sitting, holding a book, and beginning to concentrate, and to encourage the naming of objects and numbers by the beginning-to-be-verbal infant. Both kinds of books have a slick finish and can be wiped clean with a damp cloth.

In addition to the soft cloth and thick-paged cardboard

books (one of which should be a counting book), a large picture book of nursery rhymes is a must. Many kindergarten teachers sadly report that there are children coming to school who have never heard of a nursery rhyme. As the child moves through the second year of infancy, he should be introduced to picture books and illustrated storybooks.

See chapter 8, "Children's Books," for more details about what kinds of books should be introduced, and when. It is important to foster a lifelong love affair between children and the world of books as early as possible.

In getting some feel for the massive physical, psychological, and intellectual development that take place during infancy, we can begin to sort systematically through the many infant toys on the market and choose appropriate playthings for all stages. We start out with toys that stimulate the senses, toys with which the infant does not physically interact at first. Then when the child is about 4 or 5 months old, as he gains control over his body, begins grasping and sitting up, he should receive cause-and-effect toys, playthings that can be chewed on, and those that promote self-awareness.

And finally, as the child is able to move or walk on his own, has gained even more muscular control in his hands, and shows a heightened sense of awareness and interest in the world around him, he can make good use of ride-on and push toys, construction toys, puzzles, nesting objects, beginning art supplies, and infant books.

# 4
# The Childhood Years: Development and Diversity

One day a well-meaning mother bought her son eight action figures, a remote-control car, a racing set, and a pinball machine—toys and games he had seen advertised on television and had asked for. Unfortunately, she did not realize that among these purchases there was not one quiet-time toy, not one game to which her son would have to apply a good deal of mental energy or interact with others to play. Included were no books, no puzzles, no playthings that allowed him to master developmental skills, and no toys with which he could experiment and explore the world around him.

In our toy buying, we want to aim for balance and diversity. We want a good selection of both active and quiet-time toys. There should be some that the child can throw himself into physically, and also some to sit quietly with and contemplate. We should include toys that the child can play with alone as well as those that must be played with friends.

Researchers divide play and toys into a variety of categories, but there is essential agreement about the major divisions. For our purposes we shall list four broad and overlapping divisions and discuss the types of toys that fall under them: (1) toys that stimulate *symbolic play*; (2) toys that stimulate *intellectual development*; (3) toys that stimulate *physical de-*

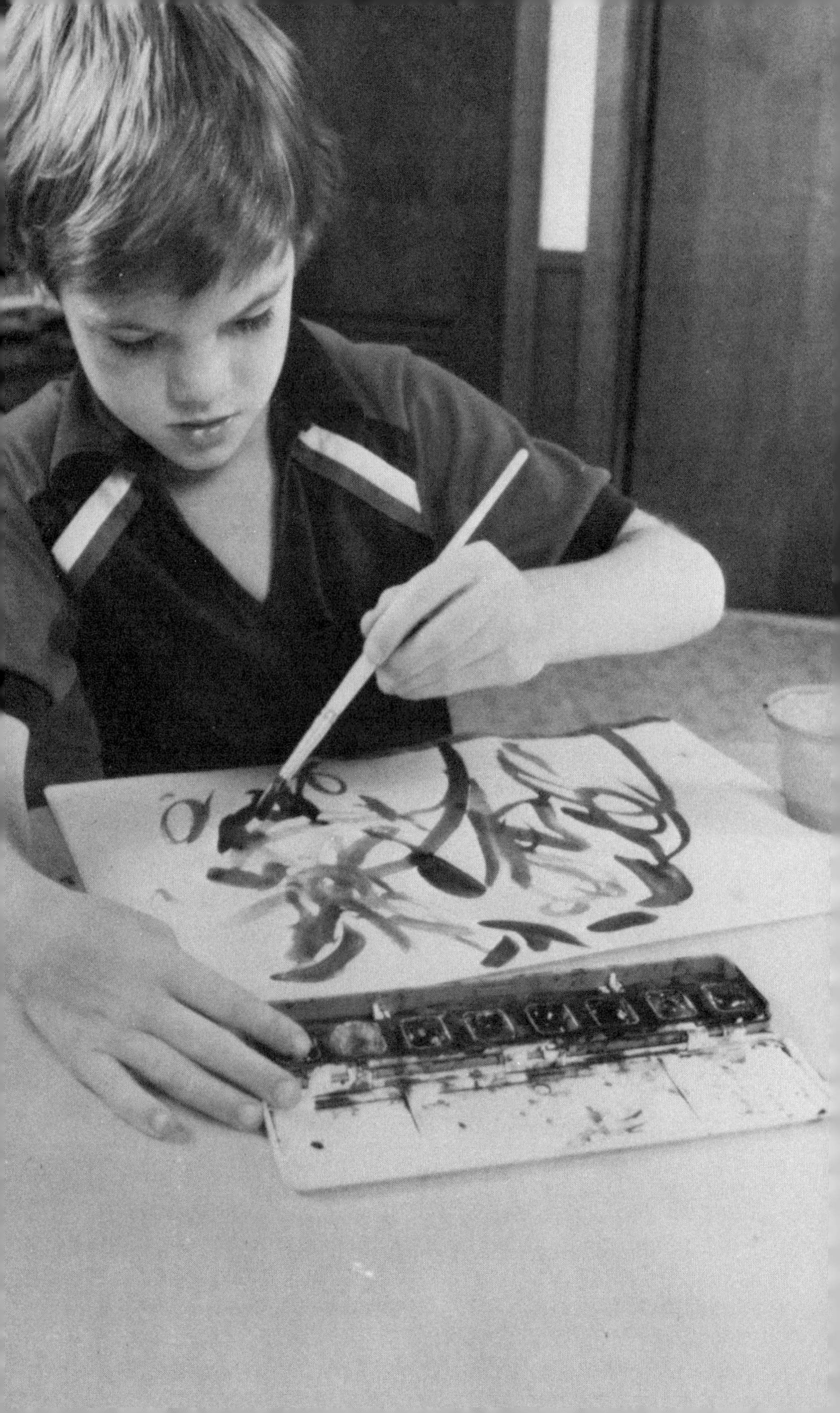

*velopment*; and (4) toys that are used to *explore, examine, and experiment.*

## Toys that Stimulate Symbolic Play

Symbolic play covers a wide range of childhood experiences in which an object, mental image, graphic rendition, or even a word is made to represent something else. "Pretend that this [a two-tiered enclosure of blocks with various toys inside of it] is the boat and that if we fall out, the sharks will get us." The blocks represent the boat, the carpet or floor is the sea, and the sharks are symbolically represented by mental images inside the children's heads. Sometimes these internal images are vivid enough to evoke some very real, very strong emotions. One mother reported that her 3-year-old was playing with his uncle, who was doing animal imitations. The uncle told the child, "Now watch, an elephant is going to come charging in here from the living room." He then put his hands to his mouth and did a realistic imitation of an elephant's trumpeting. The sound, along with the child's mental image of a charging elephant, caused him to jump up and down, screaming with fright.

Symbolic play is also at work when a child takes some blocks and "builds a car." In this case the representation is more complicated and the experience more complete—the blocks actually "become" a car because the child has constructed the seats, the dashboard, doors that open and close, and even the ignition.

Language is a system of verbal symbols that are often woven into symbolic play. Verbal sounds that the child makes as he is driving his block car or train are representative of the sounds he has heard made by the real-life object. Sometimes the child will engage in a monologue, a kind of thinking out loud in which he verbally repeats the steps and actions that he is engaging in physically.

Enriched symbolic play, language facility, and the devel-

(*Opposite*)
Photo by Larry Mulvehill, courtesy Toy Manufacturers of America

opment of cognitive skills seem to work together and facilitate each other. Before a child can pretend to be something else, he must first know something about that thing, be familiar with the sounds it makes and its other characteristics. Again we can see how a multitude of environmental experiences will provide rich material for the child's symbolic play activities. Children also need to know the difference between actually *being* something and pretending to be something. One might think that the more the child engages in fantasy play, the greater the chances are that he will begin to confuse fantasy and reality. In fact, the opposite seems to be true; the children who engage in fantasy play seem to be better able to differentiate between the two. While every child has the capacity to fantasize, many have to be encouraged to do so.

In addition, research has provided evidence that fantasy play may help in cognitive development. A group of disadvantaged preschool children who did not engage in fantasy play had gains of several IQ points on intelligence tests after they had been put into a fantasy play group where they acted out fairy tales that had been read to them.

Various creative activities such as drawing, painting, writing stories, and the like are all symbolic in that the child is producing something that is representative of his world—a story about a personal experience, a drawing of a robin that he saw on the way to school.

Musical sounds that he has heard and seeks to re-create or produce in order to symbolically represent real-life experiences are another example. The musical story of "Peter and the Wolf," in which various instruments in the orchestra represent the characters, perfectly illustrates this type of symbolism. (It is unfortunate that there are not more of these symbolic musical stories for children.)

Many kinds of construction, whether with mosaic tiles, blocks, or beads, involve symbolism. The finished structure represents something the child knows exists in the real world.

Symbolic play involves a great many imaginative, make-believe, invented situations. Sometimes the child can reconstruct and confront in symbolic play painful, frightening real-life situations, often alleviating his anxiety about them. This can readily be observed in the children's wards of hospitals, where there are dramatic productions with puppets and other activities. A child scheduled for surgery or some frightening procedure may be allowed to play with a toy hypodermic needle, stethoscope, or bandages. Playing with miniature hospitals, toy doctors and nurses, miniature operating rooms, and other equipment can allow the child to express his fears in an indirect way to the hospital staff and, in turn, be reassured by them.

Playing house or hospital, working with paper dolls, puppets, marionettes, and dollhouses, making up and carrying on dialogues with imaginary playmates—all of these tap the same creative imaginary forces and fit neatly under the heading of symbolic play.

Toys that stimulate the imagination and encourage symbolic play may be more important than was previously realized—not just in the case of artistic and creative pursuits, but in scientific areas as well. Many scientists report that their imaginations play an extremely important role in their thinking and problem solving. There has even been a reevaluation by some psychologists of the phenomenon of children's imaginary playmates. Some feel that instead of this being a somewhat "spacy" and harmful activity, imaginary playmates signal a rich fantasy life that plays its own vital role in developing creativity, and which may encourage flexibility and an ability to see many possible solutions to a problem.

In a study reported in the September 1978 issue of *Psychology Today*, some researchers at Yale found that 55 to 65 percent of the children who made up imaginary playmates "differed sharply from the rest: they were less aggressive and more cooperative; they smiled more, they showed a greater ability to concentrate; they were seldom bored; their language was richer and more advanced, especially among the boys." They also watched far less television—only half as many hours per week. And even when they did watch the screen, their

*Playing "hospital" can help alleviate fears about real-life medical situations.* Photo by Larry Mulvehill, courtesy Toy Manufacturers of America

choice of programs was quite different—they were not interested in the cartoons and violent shows that the other group preferred. Thus, while the emphasis used to be on pathology, we now see these imaginary playmates as a healthy sign. These children have the ability to create their own worlds, but they also have a strong grasp of what is reality and what is fantasy, and they can easily move from one to the other.

Some researchers who have worked in this area feel that children who have imaginary playmates tend to be very intelligent. This does not mean, however, that if your child does not make up a friend, he is less imaginative or intelligent than those who do. It is estimated that 15 to 30 percent of children between the ages of 3 and 10 years do make up imaginary playmates, with a high proportion of them being firstborns and only children. For these children, fantasy playmates serve a variety of purposes. Sometimes they are used as a scapegoat (if Johnny breaks a chair, he will say his imaginary playmate did it). Sometimes the imaginary friend will be cast in the role of the child's conscience, which tells him when he should not be doing certain things. Sometimes the friend is a confidant in stressful times, such as during the parents' divorce. Often, especially with firstborns and only children, imaginary playmates are safeguards against loneliness. When the reason for which the imaginary playmate was invented no longer exists, many times the friend will disappear. Again, we must trust the child's timing.

*"Let's-Pretend" or Fantasy Play*

Often in fantasy play, the child gets a chance to try on roles that he is learning about and preparing for, but not yet ready to assume. Some of the toys that facilitate symbolic "let's-pretend" play include:

> dolls and doll clothes (Raggedy Ann and Andy, Barbie, and other fashion dolls)
> doll carriage, walker
> dollhouse, miniature furniture, dollhouse family
> paper dolls

Colorform sets (by Colorform; pieces of thin plastic adhere to plastic playboard)
posable action figures (Superman, Spiderman, Big Jim, G.I. Joe)
playhouse, children's tent
parents' dress-up clothes
shopping cart
pots and pans
china tea set, tea cart
children's table and chairs
toy vacuum cleaner
toy mop and broom
nonelectric play iron, ironing board
toy blender, mixer
toy dryer
play refrigerator, sink, oven, nonelectric toy stove
kitchen utensils
plastic fruit, play food packages
cash register, play money
play farm and zoo with animals
play circus
play school
doctor's kit, nurse's kit
play intercom phones
walkie-talkies
hobbyhorse
stuffed animals
toy vehicles: truck, cement mixer, tractor, crane, fire engine, ambulance, etc.
fireman's hat
child's mirror (full-length)

*Creative Play—Artwork*

The minute a child says, "I'm going to make a picture," and puts some marks onto a piece of paper, he has achieved one of the most significant feats of childhood: the symbolic representation of something from an internal mental image or the external environment. Typically, the first drawings of a child in late infancy are a series of linear markings:

Then he will begin to make a circle, at first not always completely closed. Carl Jung called this "the magic circle or mandala." This circle then becomes the head of the human figure. These first drawings of people are reminiscent of a "tadpole man," as the extremities extend directly from the head, with no trunk.

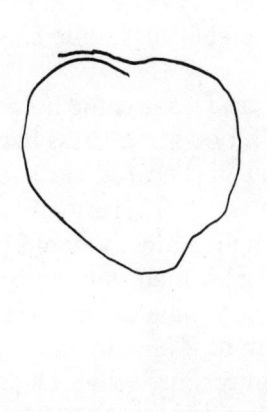

Finally, the child attempts a more realistic rendition of the human body. It is interesting that children from all cultures go through this same sequence of linear markings, circles, "tadpole men," and then more realistic human figures. From there they go on to create other representations—houses, trees, animals, the writing of words, etc. What is important for the child is the joy that comes from the *process* of painting or drawing, not the literal reproduction of real life. An interest in this will come later, around age 8 or 10. Even then it should be the result of self-discovery, and not something imposed from the outside by a parent or teacher.

Many kinds of artistic symbolic play will allow the child to experience a sense of power, to play a game of omnipotence. One mother remembers playing such a game while coloring when she was a child. She would pretend that she was a goddess, bringing the figures on the page to life by coloring them in. As she finished coloring each figure, she would make up dialogue for it. (Of course they could not move their arms and legs and mouths until they were colored in.) What a wonderful fantasy game for a child who had very little power in the real, grown-up world, but who could exercise absolute power in her own fantasy world of coloring books.

When the child has produced a piece of artwork, it should not be evaluated in adult terms. The artist should not be told, "Oh, you left the fingers off the little girl's hand, and why did you make the dog green?" Many times, we adults can unintentionally stamp out and inhibit creativity in our children.

When my second child was in first grade, she came home from school one day and told me that a boy in her class had been given a grade of "D" on a drawing because he had colored his tree orange. My response was, "Can you think of any instances when a tree might be orange?" She thought for a minute and then said, "In the fall." She then named the other fall leaf colors. Then I said, "Can you think of any other color leaves might be, or can you think of a famous painter who painted his trees a color other than green?" After a little coaxing she said, "Oh, yes, Claude Monet painted his trees pink." "Right, because that is the color they looked to him at dawn," I said. (We had seen Monet's paintings at a museum and afterward had borrowed books with reproductions of his work from the library.) "Now, if you look outside at night and it is very dark, what color do the leaves look?" "Black," was the reply. "Okay then, we know that the leaves of trees can look or be red, black, brown, green, yellow, orange, pink, and maroon, depending on the situation." "Uh-huh," she said, as she skipped off to draw a batch of pink trees.

Fortunately, there are many fairly inexpensive toys that stimulate and enhance artistic creativity in children. Crayons head the list. When buying crayons for young children up to about 4 or 5 years of age, choose those that are large and either round, hexagonal, or flat on one side. The hexagonal and flat ones will not roll. Because of their lack of small-muscle control in the fingers, young children can manipulate large crayons better. You can buy crayons in packages of from eight to 124 colors. Crayola is the brand that gives you the greatest diversity. The thirty-two-piece box comes with a durable plastic case that helps with storage. (I wonder why they don't do that for all sizes?)

Felt-tipped markers are also good; they are available in different-sized packages and range from thick to slim shapes suitable for the older child.

Clay is another very important artistic material. There are also products such as Plasticine and Pongo that come in bright colors and do not harden, so they can be used over and over again. The primary disadvantage of these is the eventual loss of color when they are mixed together. After a time, it becomes a homogenous gray, but it does remain pliant and moldable. Play-doh is reusable for a short period of time, but it does eventually harden. These sculptural materials are the ultimate in unstructured creative play—just a glob of raw material that the child molds into anything he can imagine.

We should be careful about where our children use clay. Cleanup can be difficult, to say the least. Some parents give it to their children only during the seasons they can work with it outdoors.

*Some toys and other tools that help stimulate artistic creativity:* front row, kit containing colored pencils, paints, and wax pencils; lace doilies and construction paper; crayons; acrylic paints; middle row, cup holding T-square, scissors, paintbrushes, pencils; set of watercolor paints; calligraphy pens, inks, and lettering books; pencil sharpener; felt-tipped markers; top row, modeling clay and shaping tools; glue; Papercraft *(an origami book);* Things to Make for Children *(a project book);* clear spray fixative or preservative.

The following is a list of toys and other products that encourage creative artistic play:

| | |
|---|---|
| crayons | basketmaking materials |
| felt-tipped markers | beadwork set |
| colored pencils | clay, Play-doh, Plasticine |
| drawing paper | pottery wheel |
| watercolors | sculpture kit |
| tempera paints | sewing kit |
| paintbrushes | sewing cards (a picture is |

created by pulling yarn or shoelace-type string through holes in an outline)
beginning needlepoint kit
beginning embroidery kit
weaving loom
workbench and carpentry tools
leathercraft set

easel
finger paint
scissors
paste, glue
colored construction paper
lace paper doilies
colored chalk and oil pastels
chalkboard
stenciling set
metal foil craft set
plastic craft set

As the child approaches adolescence we might add:

charcoals
acrylic and oil paints
canvases

calligraphy set
silk-screening kit

It is a good idea to keep supplies of art materials on hand at all times. Sometimes I will tell my 5-year-old, "Go make a present for me. I'm your hard-working mother and I deserve it." Often I am amazed at what I get. If you need help in thinking up artistic experiences for your children, the following books may be useful, or check your local library under the heading "Art Activities for Children."

>  Comins, Jeremy. *Art from Found Objects.* New York: Lothrop, Lee and Shepard Co., 1974.
>  Hart, Tony. *The Young Letterer.* New York: Frederick Warne and Co., 1965.
>  Kampmann, Lothar. *Creating with Colored Paper.* New York: Van Nostrand Reinhold Co., 1967.
>  Slade, Richard. *Modeling in Clay, Plaster and Papier-mâché.* New York: Lothrop, Lee and Shepard Co., 1967.
>  Weiss, Harvey. *Clay, Wood and Wire: A How to Do It Book of Sculpture.* New York: William R. Scott, 1956.

———. *Collage and Construction.* New York: Young Scott Books, 1970.

———. *Paint, Brush and Palette: The Beginning Artist's Library.* New York: Young Scott Books, 1966.

Sometimes the library will have films for loan that will illustrate various art projects children can easily do at home.

*Creative Play—Construction*

When a child uses construction toys, he is creating a structure, a configuration, whether it is a block castle or motorcycle, a mosaic ashtray or a doll's dress. The child is both engaging in symbolic play and satisfying a need to make something. His creation may be a reproduction of some object in his environment. Or he may not at first have any idea of what he is building. He is just building, enjoying the process and not visualizing the finished product. When he is older, he will announce, "I am going to build a house." He will have a mental image of a very specific structure that he will set out to reproduce.

Of course, the unstructured construction materials are best. Unstructured simply means that the toy provides the basic raw material with which the child can exercise his own particular creative urges. There are no rigid standards and no right or wrong ways to build the creation. The child has complete freedom to begin and end it at any point, and anything that he builds can have beauty and meaning.

In addition to getting experience in eye-hand coordination and discovering some very basic laws of physics, the child has the satisfaction of building something and feels a sense of power from manipulating his world.

Some of the best construction toys are:

Bristle Blocks (Playskool)
Bristle Bears (Playskool)
Lego (Lego Systems)

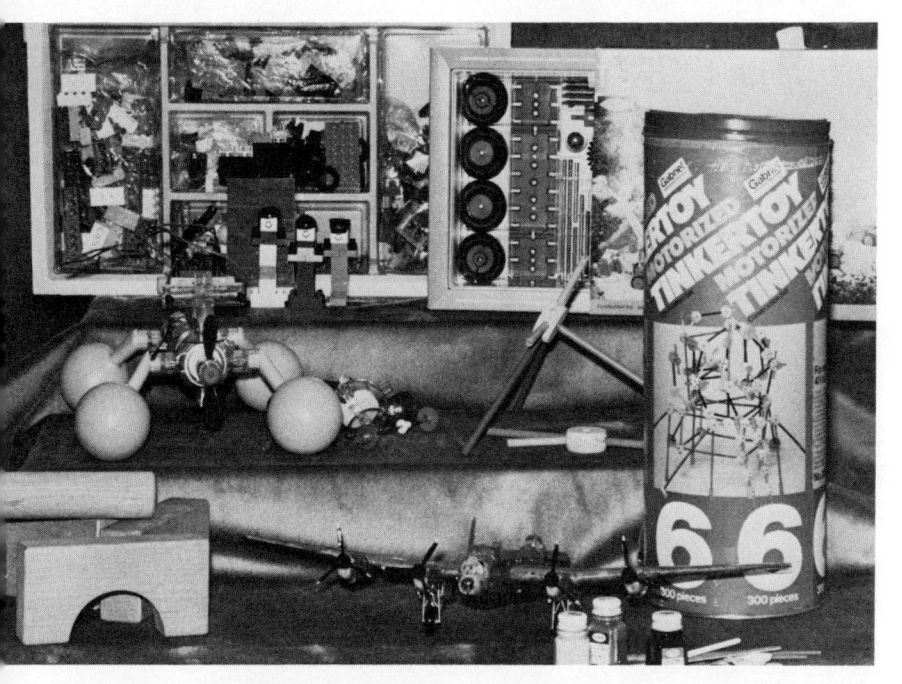

*Some toys that aid creative construction:* front row, *Playskool's Unit Blocks;* model airplane, paints, and tools; middle row, *Playjour's Capsela, Gabriel's Motorized Tinkertoys;* top row, *Entex's Loc Blocs, Fisher Technics' moving vehicles construction kits.*

    Duplo (Lego Systems)
    Capsela (Playjour)
    Ramaggon (Highland)
    Lincoln Logs (Playskool)
    Table Top Blocks, ABC Blocks, Unit Blocks (Playskool and other manufacturers)
    Constructo Straws (Parker Brothers)
    Tinkertoys (Gabriel)
    Erector Sets (Gabriel)
    Play Panels (Childcraft)
    block play people, traffic signs, vehicles, animals, trains, boats
    models of boats, cars, planes
    mosaic play tiles
    visible eight operating engine

sewing machine, material, patterns for doll clothes
large stringing beads

The level of development in the small muscles of the fingers will determine to some degree which construction toys can be used at which ages. Some brands, such as Duplo and Lego, have different-sized blocks for different ages, and the suggested ages are noted on the boxes. The larger blocks are generally for young children, while the smaller blocks are for older children who have the manual dexterity necessary to handle them.

*Creative Play—Music*

As we have seen, infants are introduced to rhythm before birth, while still in the womb, where they hear the mother's heartbeat. They are accustomed to this sound and seem to be soothed by it after birth. Studies have shown that premature infants who are placed in a nursery where a recording of the human heartbeat is played cry less, eat more, sleep more, and gain weight faster than those who do not have this advantage.

The baby is first introduced to the world of music through lullabies crooned by his parents, and through tunes from musical mobiles and stuffed animals. By his second year, the child is perfectly capable of making his *own* music with his ever-present musical instrument, his voice. He can provide his own accompaniment by clapping. It goes without saying that these musical endeavors should be applauded even though it is clear that another Grace Bumbry or Luciano Pavarotti has not yet emerged.

Parents should not wait for the schools to teach children all of the songs that they will sing. There is no reason why we can't teach them some of the nursery rhymes and songs we learned during childhood. As children get older, sing-alongs help make such tasks as cleaning the kitchen pass much faster. When driving together in the car, turn off the radio and sing till your destination.

Children will get a lot of musical enjoyment out of some of these toys:

toy piano
Kalimba (thumbnail piano)
electronic chord organ
toy drum
steel drum
tom-toms
bongo drums
harmonica
recorder
toy guitar
toy ukelele
xylophone
tambourine
triangle
zither
glockenspiel
bells
cymbals, finger cymbals
maracas
rhythm sticks
wood blocks
sandblocks
marimba
kazoos
tuning forks
music box
musical tops
musical computer toys (Mattel's Magical Musical Thing and Merlin)
records of nursery rhymes, stories, songs (Caedmon and Folkways produce excellent recordings for children)
tapes of stories, blank tapes for the child to make his own

*Creative Play—Drama*

Drama or interesting dialogue is basic to most "let's-pretend" play. It is especially emphasized when the child can "get out of himself" and speak for or become someone else, such as the mother in the dollhouse or the engineer of a train of chairs. Some toys that specifically facilitate creative dramatic play include:

> puppets and puppet theater
> marionettes and marionette theater
> Colorform sets
> old clothes, costumes
> dollhouses and miniature furniture (see chapter 6)
> paper dolls
> posable action figures

## *Toys that Stimulate Intellectual Development*

A second broad category of toys are those that directly help in the development of intellectual ability. Actually, most toys do this to some extent. Whenever a child is playing with a toy, whether it is an unbreakable mirror, a jigsaw puzzle, or a doll, he is exploring his environment and thinking, organizing, and assimilating the results of this play interaction into his own logical system. Based on his age and level of intellectual development, he may come up with some incorrect "becauses" and may draw some incorrect conclusions. Nevertheless, the *process* is systematic and logical.

When the child is participating in a dialogue with a friend or engaged in a monologue, he is developing language facility. When he tries to move a heavy block that, on the first try, does not move, and he thinks, "This block is heavy and I must push harder if I am to move it," he has discovered a basic law of physics. When he builds a block tower on a narrow base and it keeps falling until he enlarges the diameter of the base, he has discovered *on his own* a basic engineering principle.

This personal discovery is very important. It is said that "I hear and I forget. I see and I remember. I do and I understand." If someone tells him, he might forget. If he discovers it himself, it is a lesson learned for life. My 5-year-old had been playing the game Chutes and Ladders for almost two years. She could count the number of squares that she was supposed to move, but when she got to the end of the row, she didn't know which way to go and sometimes would go in the wrong direction on a new row. One day while playing the game, suddenly and with no explanation from anyone, she said, "Oh, I see, it goes like this." She pointed with her index finger in the air and traced the exact pattern of the moves on the board. From that moment of insight on, no one would have to tell her which way to move during the game. Then she said, "And this is the way you move in Candyland," tracing the correct trail for that game as well. From that first discovery she realized that many board games have a specific pattern of moves.

Some psychologists feel that if the child does not get a chance to discover things for himself, that if everything is done for him, then he will be adversely affected both intellectually and emotionally. He will doubt his own abilities. He will not feel self-confident or competent enough to initiate activities on his own, and he will not learn to become self-motivated and self-directed.

We parents need to be aware of the sequence of intellectual development so that we can provide the appropriate toys and experiences to facilitate this development. Toys that are beyond the child's capabilities will serve no useful purpose: a 100-piece jigsaw puzzle will have no meaning for a 2-year-old. Those toys that are beneath the child's developmental level will quickly bore him. Each toy must offer an appropriate challenge, one that is not overwhelming. Piaget felt that the greatest intellectual growth or stretching takes place when there is an incongruence, some element that challenges the child's view of the world. "This round piece will not fit into the square hole, it will only fit into the round one." The child may not know how to explain this situation in words, but he is learning the lesson just the same.

The more challenges we can give the child at the appropriate times; the more experiences he can have; the more discoveries he can make; the more learning that occurs through play—the greater the child's intellectual development will be.

Types of toys that facilitate the development of intellectual abilities are:

- puzzles (see chapter 7 for more about choosing these)
- board or table games (see chapter 7)
- magnetic alphabet and numbers (these can be stuck on the refrigerator and played with by the child while you are cooking dinner)
- pegboard and pegs
- stacking color cones such as Fisher-Price's Rock-A-Stack, Brio's Ring Pyramid, Childcraft's Stacking Cones
- cubical counting blocks
- abacus
- shape-sorting toys
- mosaic design tiles
- nesting blocks, cups, or cubes
- Russian Matreshka or nesting dolls
- computer toys such as Parker Brothers' Merlin, Encore's Mimic Me, and Milton Bradley's Simon
- computer programs such as Atari's Fun with Numbers, Intellivision's Brain Games
- Milton Bradley's Sequence Cards (the child arranges these in proper order to tell a story)

Toys that can be taken apart and put back together form a special category of mental development toys, those that foster the important skills of reversibility and whole-part discrimination (see page 28). In reading, the child must learn to see both the whole word and the individual letters (parts). Until he is about 5 to 7 years of age, it is most difficult for him to see

*Toys to stimulate intellectual development:* front row, *Russian Matreshka* or nesting dolls *(teach size relationships, reversibility);* middle row, stacking cups *(size relationships, reversibility);* top row, pegboard and pegs *(counting and number concepts, patterns);* shape sorter box *(matching geometric shapes).*

these both at the same time. Thus the child needs many opportunities to practice putting things together and taking them apart. This will also help in understanding fractions and other mathematical concepts. The following types of toys introduce the concepts of reversibility and whole-part discrimination:

> puzzles
> nesting cups, barrels, cubes, dolls
> play cobbler's bench

*Construction toys such as Duplo's Basic Building Set are excellent for teaching the concepts of whole-part discrimination and reversibility; they also enhance manual dexterity.* Photo courtesy Lego Systems

Also good for teaching these concepts are construction toys such as:

Duplo and Lego (Lego Systems)
Tinkertoys (Gabriel)
Table Top Blocks (Playskool and other manufacturers)
Loc Blocs (Entex)
Ramaggon (Highland)
Capsela (Playjour)
Lincoln Logs (Playskool)

## *Toys that Stimulate Physical Development*

As we have seen, physical development begins in infancy. As the baby begins to get stronger, he progresses from random, jerky, reflexive movements to conscious control of his large muscles. At each step along the way, increased physical development produces ripples in the areas of social and psychological development.

When a child "discovers" his hands, and how he can make them turn and grasp and let go, the look of rapt attention and wonder on his face is a joy to behold. When he has the physical ability to reach out and grasp a toy voluntarily, to examine it visually and put it in his mouth, he is getting valuable information about his world. He uses all of his senses to explore, discover, examine, and organize his environment.

When he can physically control his feet and legs and thereby hook a foot in his crib jungle gym, he is learning, in some rudimentary way, the principle of cause and effect, and also the idea that "*I* can produce an effect that will change the world in some way." It cannot be stressed too much how important this feeling of having some control over the environment is to a child's later feelings of self-confidence and competence. When the infant is able to sit up alone, his world is greatly expanded visually and his hands are free to explore.

As the infant moves into early childhood, he is physically participating in a much more complex and demanding world. By this time, he has developed many physical skills—walking, grasping, reaching, bending, holding, running, jumping, and dressing himself. He is also becoming more coordinated, developing the large and small muscles and also learning to use them in conjunction with the eyes.

During this time, practice is the key to the further development and refinement of physical skills. Children have a very real need for physical activity, and during early childhood, there is also an enthusiasm and unselfconsciousness about attempting new feats that further encourage practice. The repetition that is required to perfect a particular physical action soon becomes boring to an adult, but it doesn't seem to bother children as much. They delight in learning and accomplishing new feats, and we must always reinforce them in these accomplishments. When a 2-year-old shows how he can propel himself up off the floor for a split second, we must applaud. For the toddler, the accomplishment is not enough in itself; somebody must watch him perform.

As the child begins walking, push-and-pull toys foster additional practice. Toys that lead him to crawl, propel himself, lift, bend, throw, climb, carry, and run contribute to physical development and help him develop a sense of his body. He should be given some toys whose size and weight demand physical exertion, such as large building blocks, ride-on cars, toy wheelbarrows.

Around the time the child is 5 or 6 years old, and certainly by age 8 or 9, he has acquired the basic motor skills, which he will go on to refine and extend through adolescence. Physical prowess will contribute to his self-confidence and often lead to positive responses from his peers. Thus the infant should be provided almost from birth with toys and activities that call for physical activity. We must allow for the time and the space needed for practice and refinement of acquired physical skills. And we must remember to encourage and praise the child's accomplishments.

Some of the toys that enhance physical development from early childhood on are:

    ring toss
    beanbag toss
    horseshoes
    building blocks
    large hollow blocks for tugging, carrying
    large empty cartons to push, pull, climb into
    pounding toys
    toy gardening tools
    inflatable punching figures, punching bag
    boxing gloves
    hobbyhorse, rocking horse
    rocking chair
    seesaw
    jungle gym

*Marx's Big Wheels ride-on toy.* Photo by Larry Mulvehill, courtesy Toy Manufacturers of America

- balance board (you can make this yourself using a few blocks of wood and a board; it should be a few inches off the ground)
- jump rope
- trucks, cars, and other vehicles to push along (Tonka, Nylint, Flynt, Tootsie Toy, Buddie L, and John Deere make good metal ones; Fisher-Price has a line of plastic vehicles—school bus, jet—which include play people)
- train sets (both child-propelled and mechanical)
- ride-on toys that are pushed along by the child's feet (Playskool's Tyke Bike, Fisher-Price's Horse and Explorer)
- pedal ride-on toys (the Big Wheel and Little Wheel vehicles made by many manufacturers)
- scooter
- tricycle

bicycle
wagon
toy stroller, wheelbarrow, etc. (Mattel's Tuff Stuff line has some good choices)
pogo stick
hula hoop
ice skates, roller skates
bolo bat (paddle with ball attached; develops eye-hand coordination)
kite
balls of all kinds
baseball equipment
basketball
football
tennis racket, balls
badminton set
croquet set

## *Toys that Are Used to Explore, Examine, and Experiment*

Many playthings help the child explore, examine, and experiment with the world around him. They help him discover physical principles, help him learn facts, and introduce him to different disciplines and interests. They can be called "educational toys," but the children don't have to know this.

Queen Victoria's husband, Prince Albert, gave educational toys a tremendous boost because of his interest in providing the best education for their son. Children should have access to many toys of this type to ensure a well-rounded play experience. Consider some of these toys and other items:

spinning top
kite
mobile kit
globe

*Some toys used to explore, examine, experiment:* front row, *cubical counting blocks; globe; calculator; design cubes and cards;* middle row, *alphabet blocks;* top row, *number dominoes; magnifying glass.*

    protractor
    flashlight (some are self-generating and need no batteries)
    floating bath toys (remember Archimedes!)
    prism
    magnet and iron filings
    lock and key
    toy gardening tools
    models of motors, cars, boats, airplanes, etc.
    models of the human body (Visible Man, Visible Woman by Revell)
    thermometer
    weather forecasting equipment (including barometer and anemometer)

kaleidoscope
color paddles (lucite frames that show color mixing)
rock-polishing kit
scales for weighing
stethoscope
speedometer
pedometer
clock (a toy or a real one that shows the internal gears)
compass
binoculars
telescope
microscope
chemistry set
dissecting and slide-making kit
printing set
ant farm
silk factory (watching silkworms spin)
aquarium
terrarium

The following playthings provide experience in developing skills that are needed for mathematics:

Numberland game (Selchow & Righter)
clock
shape-sorting toys
magnetic arithmetic board
stopwatch
colored counting cubes
cash register, play money
shape puzzles (geometric shapes that fit together on a puzzle board)
pegs and pegboard
measuring cups and spoons from kitchen or lab
abacus
dominoes
pedometer

number puzzles (two-piece puzzles in which one half has the numeral and the other half the corresponding number of items)

Hobbies that are begun in childhood are often continued and greatly expanded on in adolescence. Sometimes they even develop into investments or career interests. Collecting dolls, miniatures, toy soldiers, matchbox cars, stamps, coins, or butterflies can be a valuable hobby, as can crafts such as doll making, clothing design, leatherwork, or woodworking. Often the child involved in a hobby will want to gather as much information as he can about it, thus gaining experience in study and research.

# 5
## Best-Loved Toys: Dolls and Stuffed Animals

### Dolls

Dolls are truly universal and have been a part of mankind's history in all cultures for centuries. Archaeological digs have produced doll figures in Europe, Africa, the Orient, and the Americas. Probably the earliest dolls were not playthings at all, but figures of some religious significance. However, a doll that did seem to have been a child's toy was found in France and dated over one million years old. The ancient Romans and Aztecs also had figures that seemed to have been used as toys.

By the 1400s there was at least one professional doll maker in business—in Nuremburg, Germany. With her master wood craftsmen and plentiful forests, Germany was the undisputed leader in the production not only of dolls but of all toys up until the two twentieth-century world wars. Most of the dolls of the sixteenth and seventeenth centuries were made of wood and had movable joints. Even in the nineteenth century, dolls tended to be a sideline of cabinetmakers.

Wood was not the only material used in making dolls. In antiquity they were made of clay, bones, and stone. Later, rawhide was also used; this attracted rats, however, and paint chipped and peeled off of it.

Wax dolls were manufactured in Germany during the 1600s, in much the same way wax museum figures are made

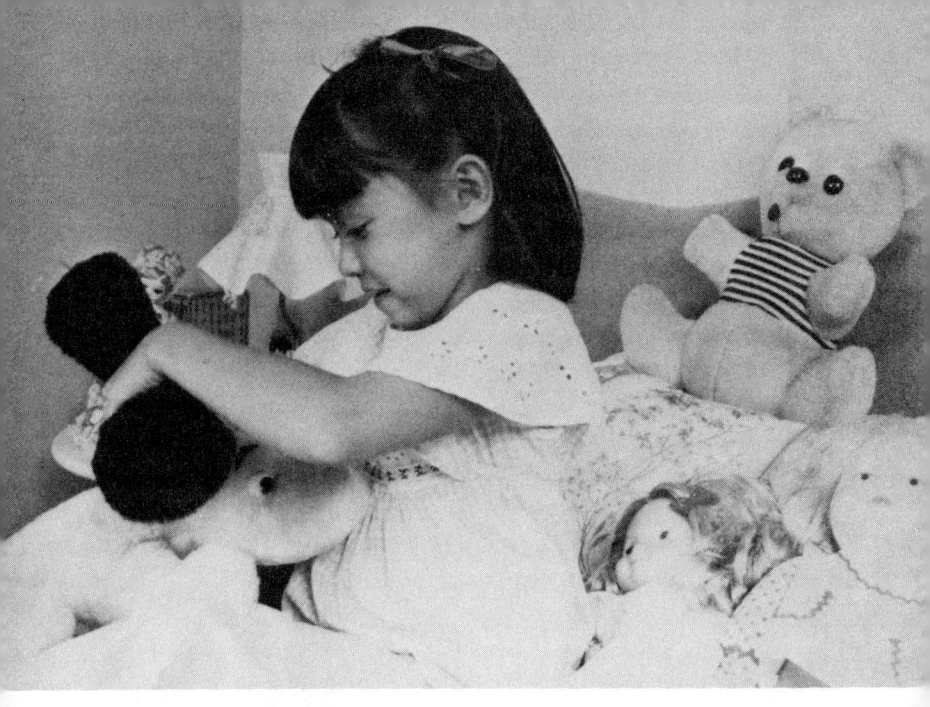

Photo by Larry Mulvehill, courtesy Toy Manufacturers of America

today. Sometimes the wax was put over a wooden cone, sometimes over papier-mâché. You can see examples of wax, bisque, and china dolls in the Smithsonian's National Museum of American History in Washington, D.C. The 1800s saw the manufacture of dolls from copper, brass, pewter, zinc, and tin. Celluloid was also used during this time, but it proved too fragile to be a mainstay in doll production.

In 1851 Nelson Goodyear, the brother of the man who invented vulcanized rubber, took out the first patent for the hard rubber used to make dolls' heads. Finally, here was a soft, lifelike material that was unbreakable and able to withstand handling by children. Today most dolls are made of vinyl—soft, smooth, lifelike plastic. The dolls are then stuffed with foam, cotton, or kapok (a silky fiber obtained from the fruit of the Malaysian silk-cotton tree).

The 1800s also saw the advent of the baby doll. Prior to this time, dolls were adult figures. There were some dolls in the 1700s that seemed to represent children, but since their dress was a replica of adult dress and children were treated as miniature adults, it was difficult to tell whether the dolls were supposed to be children or adults. Today a large portion of the doll market is made up of dolls that represent infants and small children.

Walking and talking dolls were available by the 1800s. One doll that we know of said "Mama" when its right hand was touched and "Papa" when its left was touched. This mechanism was patented in 1824 by Johann Matzel, who also invented the metronome.

Thomas Edison invented a talking doll that contained a phonograph on which several different discs could be played. They were very expensive, and this probably prevented their large-scale production. Now, of course, there are numerous talking dolls, saying as little as one word or as much as complete sentences.

How should you approach choosing a doll for your own children? Once you are aware of the different levels of quality that are available, and the kinds of dolls that are appropriate for a particular age or stage of development, this becomes easier than you might think.

## *Infancy (Birth–2 Years Old)*

The very first doll should probably be a rag doll. It should be small, soft, "mouthable," patterned, cuddly, and completely washable. The facial features should be embroidered or dyed-in-the-fabric so that there is no danger of the baby swallowing smooth button eyes or noses.

Fisher-Price's Cholly and Lolly dolls are excellent choices for an infant. Not only are they the right size for an older infant to hold and chew on, they are washable and have a bright gingham-patterned design, which is more interesting and attractive to the baby than a plain, solid color.

As your child moves into the second year of infancy, you might buy a "cause-and-effect" doll—one that will squeak when your baby squeezes it. Fisher-Price's Pillow dolls meet these requirements.

The child could also make good use of a small, sturdy, unbreakable vinyl doll at this time. This doll should have molded vinyl hair, as it will still be chewed on sometimes. A sewn-on "wig" would be entirely unsatisfactory for a doll that may be put into the infant's mouth.

The clothes on this type of doll can also be molded because there is no need for removable garments at this age. Typically, 2- and 3-year-olds will strip their dolls of every item of clothing. As one boy told his younger sister, "Kelly, you always dress your dolls nude."

*Dolls for Boys*

Perhaps this is the best place to address briefly the subject of boys and dolls. After infancy, when dolls begin to play a significant role in "let's-pretend" play, they have been traditionally regarded as playthings for girls—and that is why in the rest of this chapter the pronoun "she" is most often used. To do otherwise would be unnecessarily jarring. I do not mean, however, to exclude boys from the enjoyment of dolls and playing house. In this day of evolving family roles and increased participation in child rearing by fathers, playing with dolls is a valuable preparation for future role taking.

A number of dolls, such as Big Jim and GI Joe, are manufactured specifically for boys (though the manufacturers might prefer not to call them dolls). Baby dolls have tended to be overwhelmingly female, though recently there have been some available that are "anatomically correct," which means they have a penis. In his 1973 book *The Doll*, Carl Fox says:

> We owe its release to those sexually emancipated French who distributed in the United States the "anatomically correct" boy doll Petit Frère, or Little Brother. Designed by Mme. Refabert and manufactured by her husband, Claude, Little Brother had as its source of inspiration Verrocchio's statue of a cherub in the Palazzo Vecchio in Florence. In physical detail, the Little Brother doll is all

boy. *This abrupt departure from neuter Kewpie-doll bodies, which we've all grown used to from time immemorial, may shock some adult shoppers taken unawares.*

Of course, if a boy does not want to play with dolls—and many don't, after they reach a certain age—he should not be forced to. We should respect the wishes and needs of the child wherever possible.

The issue of boys playing with dolls is delightfully dealt with in a picture book by Charlotte Zolotow called *William's Doll*. When children have a clear sense of identity, and are not stifled by strictures of one kind or another, then we can choose boys based primarily on their interests, whatever they may be—not on their gender.

## Early Childhood (2–6 Years Old)

As the child moves into early childhood, the doll begins to assume a more prominent role in play activities. The child imputes more important characteristics to the doll; it becomes a "real baby." It assumes a significant role as the child moves into the fantasy world of "let's pretend." The parents must acknowledge the doll and sometimes "doll sit" or otherwise interact with it.

During this period, the child demands more complexity in the doll—babies that can drink and wet, hair that can be combed and styled, clothes that can be changed, bodies that can change positions to sit or sleep, and so on.

Accessories such as bottles, clothing, diapers, beds, blankets, trunks, and carriages become necessary accompaniments to play. In fact, much of the social play life of this age group is centered around "playing house," with the primary character being the "baby." Even when she is engaged in solitary play, the girl, during this age, may keep her doll with her much of the time. At night, she may go through the ritual of "dressing" the doll for bed, wanting the doll to sleep with her, or rigging up some complex apparatus so that the doll can sleep near her

*This group of dolls illustrates a representative baby doll, rag doll, fashion doll, and collector's doll.*

bed. She may spend a great deal of time organizing and arranging the doll's accessories.

Often a great deal of time and consideration will be given to choosing an appropriate name for the doll. The doll takes on an identity. Rarely will the child refer to it as "my doll" but rather by its name or as "my baby."

Although the children of this age group primarily prefer

the baby doll, as they near the end of this period (about 6 years) they become acquainted with the older "girl" doll. The girl doll is proportioned like a child—longer and leaner rather than having the shorter, more rounded proportions of the infant. Sometimes the child will role play with this doll, having her become a particular character with the child speaking through her in a play situation.

The fashion doll or elaborately costumed collector's doll is not a good choice for this age group. A 5-year-old will become extremely frustrated and irritated when she cannot fasten a Barbie doll's tiny shoes and garments. Watch and see how quickly the head or a limb is permanently broken off. Fashion dolls of this kind are more suitable for children age 8 and above.

Many of the dolls made by companies such as Effanbee, Ideal, Knickerbocker, Madam Alexander, Shindana, Uneeda, Fisher-Price, Horsman, Mattel, and Vogue are suitable for ages 2–6.

## Late Childhood (6–12 Years Old)

During the first part of this period—ages 6, 7, 8—a child may still spend considerable time playing with baby dolls, engaging in the many activities that go into taking care of a baby. As she gets a bit older, her interest will probably enlarge to include fashion dolls and, later, collector's dolls. By the time she is 11 or 12 years old, she will have stopped playing with the "baby" and will most likely spend her time with miniature dolls in a dollhouse, with fashion dolls, and perhaps with collectibles.

As noted earlier, fashion dolls such as Mattel's Barbie and Ken are appropriate for girls about age 8 and up. With their long, slim bodies, adult proportions, and fragile construction, these dolls are not suited to younger children.

Though many companies are introducing their own lines of fashion dolls, Mattel's Barbie and her friends—including British Barbie, Black Barbie, Spanish Barbie, Italian Barbie, Malibu Barbie, Roller Skating Barbie, Beauty Secrets Barbie,

Ken, Sindy, and Starr—are the undisputed leaders of the league. All of the dolls have extensive wardrobes of outfits and accessories that can be purchased separately. For example, Sindy has a riding outfit, her own thoroughbred horse, and a horse care set. While the accessories may be used interchangeably, the outfits are often proportioned to fit only one type of doll: Barbie clothes will fit any Barbie but are not proportioned to fit Sindy. Parents should keep this in mind when making additional accessory purchases. For the Barbie dolls, there is also an array of town houses, dream houses, vans, airplanes, sports cars, campers, and pieces of furniture that can be purchased separately.

As your child develops an interest in fashion dolls, be sure there is a place to store the accessories, and teach your child to keep them there. As one mother of a young Barbiephile said, "You don't know what real pain is until you walk into a room barefoot and step on one of those razor-sharp little high-heeled shoes that is buried in the carpet."

Some parents complain that there is an overemphasis on television and movie stars with these dolls (for example, Ideal's Loni Anderson doll). They also question the ostentatious lifestyle suggested by the array of outfits and flashy accessories. The clothes are expensive and accessories such as the tiny plastic shoes look cheap, are difficult to manipulate, and tend to break easily. Despite these objections, though, fashion dolls seem to be the perennial favorites of older girls, who sometimes delight in making their costumes themselves. If they want to do this, patterns for all types of doll clothes are available from the major pattern manufacturers. And for the preadolescent girl, Barbie dolls do offer an opportunity to try out roles and act out situations she is as yet unprepared for, but will be experiencing in a few years—in the teenage world of dating.

## Mechanical Dolls

There is a wide selection of mechanical dolls that perform various realistic activities. Kenner's Baby Alive, for example, "eats" artificial food. (If you get this one, be sure to warn your child that the doll does not eat real food!) Others talk when you pull a string, walk, get diaper rash, hold their heads for a kiss, crawl, dance, and perform many other feats. These typically are the dolls that are heavily promoted in the media, especially on television. These are the ones that children say they want Santa Claus to bring. Any one of them may be the "star" on Christmas Day, but some parents report that the interest is not sustained throughout the year, as it is with the simple baby dolls. It is also very frustrating when a mechanical doll breaks down or does not work properly.

Mattel's Dancerella, a battery-operated doll that pirouetted while you held her by her crown, was the big "star" a few Christmases ago. Of course, nobody mentioned that as soon as her hair was pulled loose (as often happened with 4-, 5-, and 6-year-olds), it would catch in the crown and have to be cut each time and then painstakingly removed. After a while, when I heard an ear-piercing "Mommy," I just grabbed my scissors and rushed to the scene. So if you are going to buy a primarily mechanical doll, buy a soft, cuddly, simple one also. It may not get much attention on Christmas Day, but it will be loved and played with throughout the year.

## Choosing Dolls

Here are some tips to help you judge the quality of a doll. When you are buying, though, always consider the age level and interests of the child you are giving it to.

1. Know something about brand names when you walk into a store. Some of the brands at the very top are Madam Alexander, Effanbee, Corolle, Sebino, Zapf, Kathy Kruze, Sasha, Peggy Nisbet, Calico Kids, Lenci, and Alresford. These dolls are, of course, the most expensive. But they also tend to last the longest and if you're planning ahead to when you or your child become collectors, you might feel that they are a worthwhile investment.

A good medium-priced doll may fit your needs, and there are a number of these available. They are manufactured by companies such as Vogue, Fisher-Price, Shindana, Mattel, Horsman, Uneeda, Ideal, and Knickerbocker.
2. Check out the "spectacular" mechanical dolls carefully. Sometimes, as with new automobiles on the market, they have flaws.
3. Check the eyes. The least expensive dolls tend to have eyes that have been spray painted on. The middle group will have "glass" eyes that remain open. The best dolls have eyes that open and close.
4. Hair is another key to the quality of a doll. Most of the dolls for older children have "rooted" hair, which has been stitched to the doll's scalp. The better-quality dolls will have the hair stitched all over the scalp rather than in patches or in a thin line down the center. There will be no large areas of bare scalp showing, and the hair will be evenly distributed over the head.
5. The doll's weight is also generally an indication of quality, with substantial heaviness being a good sign. Check to see if the arms and legs as well as the body are stuffed—although most vinyl dolls have hollow arms and legs.
6. Look at the doll's dress and determine if it is well made. Has attention been paid to detailing? What kind of fabric has been used? The answers to questions such as these help reinforce your hunch about a particular doll.

## **Stuffed Animals**

Stuffed animals run the gamut from afghans to zebras. Most animals that one can think of—both real and mythical, including dragons and unicorns—have probably been rendered in plush. They can be a few inches in size to more than 5 feet and they come in every imaginable color. Their owners range in age from the 3-week-old infant to the never-totally-grown-up adult collector.

Probably the best known and loved stuffed animal of all is the Teddy Bear. Especially in Russia, England, and Germany, stuffed bears had been known long before the appearance of Teddy's bear in 1903. However, these bears (frequently called Bruins) tended to be more ferocious in appearance and were not as cuddly and lovable as the Teddy came to be.

The Teddy Bear got its name from an incident involving the twenty-sixth president of the United States, Theodore Roosevelt. In 1902, Roosevelt went to Mississippi to settle a dispute concerning the boundary line between Mississippi and Louisiana. Being a sportsman of some note, he went on a hunting trip while he was there. He was about to shoot a bear when he realized that it was only a cub and he refrained. A political cartoonist named Barryman, who was with the now-defunct *Washington Star*, came up with a cartoon of the president turning his back on the cub. The caption read, "Drawing the line in Mississippi."

This cartoon was picked up by several newspapers around the country and provided inspiration for a Russian immigrant by the name of Morris Michtom, who was the proprietor of a small toy store in Brooklyn, New York. He made up a small brown plush bear and placed it in his store window along with a sign that read, "Teddy's Bear." Realizing that he probably needed the president's consent to attach his name to the toy, Michtom wrote to President Roosevelt to ask permission. Roosevelt assented, the bears became a big sensation, and Michtom subsequently began the Ideal Toy Company. Ideal considers itself the originator of the Teddy Bear and not too long ago reissued the "1978 Collector's Edition of the Original Ideal Teddy Bear."

While Ideal rightly lays claim to being the first company to manufacture Teddy Bears, it was not the only one to do so. A German firm called Steiff, which was well known for its excellent stuffed animals, also began to make Teddy Bears.

Steiff was started by a woman named Margarete Steiff, who in 1849, at the age of 2, had become a victim of polio. Her incapacitation may have contributed to what was at first a hobby—making small plush animals for the neighborhood children. The animals were so delightful that soon adults began buying the toys and her reputation spread. Her brother convinced her to take some of her wares to one of the toy fairs for which Germany was famous. She did, and based on this initial success, the Margarete Steiff company was born.

Whatever the original incident, since the early 1900s Steiff has been a producer of Teddy Bears and other stuffed animals of the highest quality. The Steiff company trademark is a *Knopf im Ohr*, or a button sewn in the ear of each stuffed animal.

Though Teddies and, more recently, the jelly belly and potbelly bears make the bear the most frequently seen stuffed animal, many others are available. Any type of stuffed animal can serve some of the same functions as dolls—they can be held, cuddled, talked to, taken to bed, dressed and undressed, served tea, and so on. This is especially true for many boys who, although they might ordinarily shun dolls, will faithfully take off the outfits on their stuffed Snoopys, put them into nightcaps and shirts, and tuck them tenderly into bed every night.

The age of the child for whom the toy is being purchased is an important consideration. For the few-week-old newborn, the noninteractionary plush toys such as Eden's Wagging Musicals are good. As the child begins handling the toy, the soft plush will be a "touch treat"—but it is not a particularly good candidate for mouthing. Hairy or furry plush toys should be given to the child after he has stopped putting everything into his mouth.

The realistic stuffed toys such as the mother-and-baby bears, foxes, and kangaroos are good choices for the older toddler. Stuffed toys for the young child should be completely machine washable and have riveted rather than glued-on eyes and noses. (American-made stuffed toys must meet Consumer Product Safety Commission standards regarding the amount of stress and pressure necessary to remove the eyes and noses.)

Stuffed animals with removable clothes and additional outfits are most suitable for the period of early childhood when the child has the small-muscle development and manual dexterity to handle changes in clothing. As the child moves through late childhood into adolescence, the interest in stuffed toys may wane or grow into that of the serious collector. If this happens, the limitations on the number and type of stuffed animals are determined solely by space and one's pocketbook.

If you want to buy stuffed animals based on characters in children's literature, there are:

- Michael Bond's Paddington Bear (Ganz)
- Charles Schultz's Snoopy, and other characters (Knickerbocker)
- Beatrix Potter's Peter Rabbit, and others (Eden)
- A. A. Milne's Winnie the Pooh (Mighty Star for Sears)
- Maurice Sendak's Wild Things (Colorforms)
- H. A. Rey's Curious George (Knickerbocker)

Manufacturers of popular stuffed animals include:

| | |
|---|---|
| Anima | Ideal |
| California Stuffed Toys | Kenner |
| Dakin | Knickerbocker |
| Eden | Steiff |
| Fisher-Price | Trupa |
| Ganz | |

Anima, Steiff, and Trupa are imports (Anima is from France, Steiff from Germany, and Trupa from Italy). Fisher-Price is a recent entry into the stuffed-animal arena. While their mother-

and-baby bears are adequate, they are not as vibrant and realistic as are the mother-and-baby series by California Stuffed Toys. In my opinion, Eden, California Stuffed Toys, and Atlanta Novelty have the greatest diversity and make the most delightful stuffed animals in the mid-price range. Of course, if money is no object, there is always Steiff.

# 6
# The Miniature World of Dollhouses

Dollhouses and the collecting of miniatures are extremely popular once again. It is estimated that miniatures collecting is the fastest-growing family hobby in the United States today. Like dolls, dollhouses have been around a long time and have a fascinating history. They have been found in almost every culture. Archaeologists working in northern Africa have discovered ancient miniature models of bakeries, breweries, houses, granaries, weavers' shops, gardens, and carpentry shops. The question still remains, however, whether these were actual "dollhouses" used as toys by children or whether they served some religious or funerary purpose. Since many of these objects were found in tombs, some feel that they represented important situations a person would meet after death. The assumption is that the miniatures were put there to be of service to the deceased in the afterlife, which was so important to peoples such as the ancient Egyptians. Others feel that even if they started out serving solely a religious or funerary purpose, children, upon seeing them, would have been interested and delighted by these tiny replicas, and would have soon started playing with them.

The origin of the dollhouse as a plaything is also uncertain. It is said to have been invented in both Germany and Holland. Whatever the country of its origin, it probably did not emerge as a toy until the sixteenth century. The harshness of life during medieval times precluded much attention being spent on the development of elaborate toys. Medieval children had to content themselves with objects such as spinning tops, whistles, drums, cymbals, dolls, and clay marbles that were called basses or bonces. We do know that a dollhouse was constructed for the Duke of Saxony's daughter in 1558.

Even when it was built for a child, the dollhouse was probably primarily for looking at rather than playing with—as many dollhouses are today. There is evidence that during the 1600s, some people collected the miniature houses and furnishings as a hobby. This was probably a very expensive pastime then, as it is today. It was overwhelmingly a hobby of the rich, as many utensils and pieces of furniture were handmade of silver. Some of the most extensively furnished dollhouses belonged to the children of royalty. In fact, silver miniatures were considered quite suitable toys for princes and princesses. A young prince might have a complete army of miniature silver soldiers on horses and in various states of battle dress. His play with these toys was meant to help prepare him for his future role as leader of his country's army.

The dollhouse made its popular debut in various cultures during the 1600s and 1700s. It is fortunate that many of them have been well preserved because they accurately mirrored daily life in their respective home cultures. Indeed, the furniture as well as the actual structure of the dollhouse was influenced by the particular culture in which it was produced.

In Germany (the undisputed toy manufacturing leader until World War I), the earliest dollhouses resembled cabinets. They had hinged doors that opened to reveal the interior of the house. When the dollhouse was not being used, it could be completely closed and locked, rather than one side being permanently open as is typical of dollhouses today. These cabinet dollhouses faithfully reproduced the architecture of the period, and when closed, they were accurate replicas of houses. Initially, dollhouses and their miniature furnishings were not made by toy makers; they were produced by craftsmen who did miniatures only as a sideline to their full-scale work. An architect would design the houses; cabinetmakers would make the furnishings; potters would make the dishes; and silversmiths would make some of the ornamental pieces. In fact, there was a strict guild system in Germany that prohibited one craftsman from doing the job of another, even in miniature. The dollhouses varied in structure and detail depending on the wealth of the purchaser. It is clear that they were made primarily for children, but they stimulated a great deal of interest in adults as well.

Holland, which also claims to be the originator of the

dollhouse as a toy, contributed a particular kind of cabinet dollhouse. Instead of looking like an architectural miniature, these were more like elegant pieces of furniture. With the doors closed, there were no miniature windows, shutters, or other architectural features visible on the exterior. The doors were sometimes inlaid with ivory or amber; they might even have been covered with a mural painted by a fashionable artist of the day. The cabinet was revealed as a dollhouse only when its doors were opened and the rooms outfitted with miniature furnishings were visible.

In France, the dollhouse developed during the seventeenth century. The furnishings echoed the delicately carved styles predominant during that period. Alongside the development in France of the multiroomed dollhouse came the phenomenon of the single room. There were single-roomed bedrooms, kitchens, living rooms, and even lawyer's offices, butcher shops, hat shops, and dress shops, all designed in exquisite detail. One particular vignette that was seen quite frequently was a miniature lying-in room, complete with mother figure, bed, dresser and dressings, midwife, and baby.

In England, the development of dollhouses paralleled that seen in other countries. There they were also called baby houses. Some of the most detailed and well-preserved examples were designed for royalty and the nobility. Probably the most elaborate and luxurious English dollhouse was the one presented to Queen Mary, the grandmother of the present Queen of England, in 1924. It was designed by a prominent architect of the day, Sir Edward Lutens. Although made of wood, it has the appearance of stone. It is a realistic-looking four-sided building when closed. The sides of the dollhouse are raised by electricity. There are lights throughout the house. The plumbing system is complete with hot and cold running water. Accurate detail was carried out in the furnishings, wall and window treatments, and in all of the accessories. The furniture was produced by the most famous craftsmen of the day. Even the miniature china was specially commissioned. Celebrated painters contributed miniature art masterpieces.

Prominent writers and musicians contributed literary works and musical compositions that were then reduced. The small books that filled the library were, of course, bound in real leather. The fleet of miniature cars in the garage under the house included a Rolls-Royce. There was even vintage wine in the tiny bottles stored in the wine racks in the cellar. Miniature replicas of some of the crown jewels were kept in a tiny locked safe, and as no royal English mansion would be complete without a garden, that too was included. Today this elegantly appointed, accurately detailed miniature mansion is one of the most popular tourist attractions at Windsor Castle.

America also has its share of historic dollhouses, the most famous probably being the one located at the Smithsonian Institution in Washington, D.C. This is the twenty-three-room home of "The Doll Family." Mr. and Mrs. Doll, with their several children and servants, enjoy every turn-of-the-century convenience imaginable. If you concentrate for a period of time on the richly detailed interiors of the house—the nursery and nurse's room, the children's rooms, the grand parlor, the kitchen, the library—you can begin to feel what it was like being a member of a fairly large, upper-class family around the turn of the century. Not only does the house accurately mirror a certain style of life, it also reflects some of the holiday traditions of the time. At Christmas, for example, the house stands decorated in all of its holiday splendor. One supposes that after the holidays, the miniature decorations are packed in boxes and stored away in the tiny attic until the following year.

The Doll Family and their residence were the culmination of the lifelong hobby of Miss Faith Bradford of Washington, D.C. The project was begun in 1887 and considered completed some sixty-four years later. It was presented to the Smithsonian in 1951. No miniatures enthusiast should miss visiting the Doll Family at the Smithsonian's National Museum of American History or the privately owned Washington Doll House and Toy Museum.

Although initially most of the dollhouses in America were imported from Europe, by the late 1800s and early 1900s some were being produced locally by such companies as Bliss, Converse, and Schoenhut. The American manufacturers of dollhouses, as well as other toys, received a tremendous boost as a result of embargoes placed on German imports during the two world wars.

The postwar era brought some dramatic changes to the world of dollhouses and miniatures available on the mass market. Increasingly, lithographed metal houses and molded plastic or metal furniture, rather than wooden pieces, were seen. These were machine-made, less expensive, and therefore more accessible to a larger number of children. The metal houses, which did not have three-dimensional architectural details, were a significant step backward in terms of design quality and realism, in my opinion, and the 1950s saw a decrease in demand. Then in the sixties and seventies, as already noted, there was a great revival of interest in dollhouses and miniatures, sparked as much—or more—by the adult collector as by the child; and today we see again finely crafted, realistic pieces.

Dollhouses and their furnishings are now a primary focus of attention at many stores. Large, wooden, intricately detailed houses, millinery shops, grocery stores, and butcher shops are available, as are do-it-yourself kits for both buildings and furniture. Publications such as *Nutshell News* and *Miniature Collector* are appearing on the shelves along with massive catalogs containing every imaginable miniature piece. Dollhouse museums, such as the one in Washington, have opened across the country, and annual miniatures conventions and fairs are a regular part of the local scene in many areas.

## Choosing a Dollhouse

There are many preliminary stages to go through before arriving at anything like an elaborately furnished twelve-room Victorian mansion. We can start our children out at age 2 with small, compact, unbreakable structures that have just a few rooms, several pieces of plastic furniture, and a small set of plastic people and animals. These might be other types of buildings besides houses, and they might be made of soft materials, wood, or rigid plastic.

Some excellent softly sculptured dollhouses and other buildings are Fisher-Price's The Woodsey's Store, Airport, Log House. The more rigid structures include:

- Duplo's Playville Nursery School, Playville Farm
- Sunshine's Family Playhouse
- Hasbro's Weebles Tree House
- Fisher-Price's Play Family Farm, House, Car, and Camper, Parking Garage and Service Center

When the child moves from preschool into the 5-to-8-year-old age bracket, there are a number of very satisfactory, fairly realistic dollhouses and furniture available. These include:

- Fisher-Price Doll House
- Tomy Small House and Garden
- Lundby of Sweden Doll House

Fisher-Price's plastic four-rooms-and-bath dollhouse has ten sets of furniture accessories that outfit as many as seven different kinds of rooms. It features battery-powered lighting units—tiny lights that plug into a piece of the miniature furniture. In this way the house can be lighted without complete electrical wiring.

Tomy's Small House and Garden is a relatively new addition to the world of dollhouses. It is a two-story modern house with a light, airy, realistic look. The furniture can be purchased separately, in sets. It fits in easily with the house and is as realistic as plastic furniture can be.

The Lundby house with plastic furniture accessories is also more than adequate for 5- to 8-year-olds.

When your child is about 8, you can then move into the world of real miniatures. Of course, some parents buy the plastic Barbie dollhouse for children of this age. It is purely a matter of preference, but if your child is still interested in dollhouses, why not invest in a real wooden house that may one day become a family heirloom?

In this arena, size, design, and intricacy are limited only by your finances. You can pick out a single room or a four-story mansion. Furniture kits and miniature tools are available for the do-it-yourselfer. Coordinated fabric, wallpaper, and carpeting can be put in. Miniature building materials, such as precut boards, bricks, shingles, parquetry floors, and windows, are available if you want to tackle the task of building a dollhouse or adding to the architectural detailing of a ready-made one. There are many books on miniatures decorating, window treatments, and related topics to consult for inspiration. You might also pick up one of the publications designed for miniatures collectors, such as *Nutshell News* and *Miniature Collector*; one issue contains enough advertisements for catalogs, kits, and furniture to start you on your way. If you cannot locate a miniatures store in your area, these publications usually include mini-directories that may help.

I could hardly wait until my oldest daughter reached age 8 so that real collecting could begin. When some of the local toy stores had miniature furniture on sale, I got some and rushed back to set it up in our dollhouse. On a subsequent trip to the Washington Doll House and Toy Museum, my daughter picked out an elegant pink wallpaper for the dining room, and a pattern for the nursery. The pink wallpaper sent us to the fabric store for matching pink velvet ribbon to recover the dining room chairs. My younger daughter, then 4 years old, and 11-year-old son were also delighted with the project. The girls' brother was as actively involved in where to put the furniture as they were. (Because he was not interested in "playing with a dollhouse," he called it "choosing the pieces and organizing them.")

It's easy to see the advantages boys can derive from the hobby, including an interest in collecting, architecture, interior design, carpentry, and so on. Many of the best miniatures craftsmen are men. Boys should certainly be encouraged to become involved with miniatures, and more should be done with stores, hunting lodges, and other buildings not solely identified with "dolls."

The major problem with fine wooden furniture is that it is delicate. There is no way to avoid this because of the scale on which it is created. I thought at first that a 4-year-old was too young to handle the furniture; however, mine had no difficulties. The children quickly learned that they could play, but they had to do so carefully and not treat the furniture roughly.

The younger children, with their insistence on realism, will probably demand a dollhouse family. Why have a dollhouse if there is no one living in it? They want an active home, not a lot of museum pieces. The doll family will be handled more than the furniture, so these figures should be very sturdily constructed. Two members of our first dollhouse family lost their heads and revealed nail-like pointed spikes protruding from the neck. Needless to say, they were quickly replaced. The next family was of single-unit construction, with bendable limbs and no joints.

Once your children get involved in collecting furnishings for a dollhouse, they may well be engrossed in it through the teenage years and beyond. Making furniture from kits, needlepointing tiny rugs, sewing draperies—these are all activities that may grow to be lasting interests.

# 7
# Puzzles and Games

### *Puzzles*

Some of the most inexpensive, underrated, valuable toys around are puzzles. They provide excellent opportunities for the development of intellectual skills that will be of prime importance in later life. They truly span the years from infancy to adulthood.

One Sunday I took my children over to the Archaeological Museum in Alexandria, Virginia. The Smithsonian Institution was sponsoring a special program for children in which an archaeologist spoke about some digs that were currently being excavated in Alexandria. In an easy-to-understand, informal presentation, he explained what an archaeologist does and why the work is important. He showed slides of work in progress and talked about the procedures used to recover American colonial artifacts. Samples of toys that had been discovered were passed around and examined by the children. The cleaning process was described in response to one curious youngster's question. Later the children learned a colonial marble game using some of the excavated clay marbles. We looked at the artifacts on display and then wandered over to a table on which there were hundreds of pieces of broken crockery. The staff allowed the children to carefully try to fit some pieces together. It occurred to me then that a child who was excellent at and experienced with jigsaw puzzles would certainly have an easier time with this sort of work than one who was not. So if you think you may be bringing up a future archaeologist, be sure to supply your child with lots of jigsaw puzzles to be worked.

One of the most important skills that is developed by working with puzzles is that of *sensory-motor coordination*. Many researchers on infancy and childhood, including Jean Piaget, feel that children are not born with a preformed chunk of intelligence located somewhere in the brain; they feel that the origins of intelligence (influenced, of course, by the interaction of heredity and the prenatal environment) are rooted in the concept of sensory-motor coordination. This is a complex-sounding term meaning that when an infant sees, hears, tastes, smells, or feels something, he will make a physical muscular, or motor, response to it on the basis of that particular sensory experience. These sensory-motor coordinations become the building blocks of intelligence. The motor responses made later on to particular sensory events will be based on the child's past experiences. For example, after seeing his crib gym many times, a child will immediately put a foot into one of the rings and shake it vigorously. This response would not occur if he had never seen a crib gym before.

One current theory concerning the workings of the brain says that every sensory experience a person has is stored somewhere in the brain as a physical or electrical trace. According to this theory, a child will not be very intelligent or richly creative if he has not had the varied experiences thought to provide the bedrock for the development of intelligence and creativity.

Puzzles give the child much practice with one form of sensory-motor coordination, that of eye-hand coordination. The child spots the right puzzle piece and, processing this visual information in his brain, makes the motor response of picking it up and placing it in its proper position.

Puzzles also help in:

- seeing spatial relationships—"seeing" abstractly in the mind that a particular piece fits in a certain spot
- developing powers of concentration
- increasing attention span—the ability to work for a long time at a particular activity
- exercising small muscles located in the fingers
- improving visual scanning—involving the small muscles of the eyes. This is an important skill in reading, as the eyes must move back and forth across the lines continuously. Some researchers are concerned that children who watch a lot of television do not get enough prereading scanning exercise.
- developing problem-solving skills. Each time the child fits in a piece, he is solving a "mini-problem" that will contribute to the solution of the overall puzzle. Children get a tremendous feeling of accomplishment at finishing a puzzle, whether it is a 2-year-old completing a four-piece puzzle or a 10-year-old finishing one with 500 pieces.

*Choosing Puzzles*

Wooden puzzles are excellent ones to begin with as they tend to have larger, thicker pieces and can be more easily handled. They are also very sturdy and can stand up to years of repeated use. Fisher-Price and Playskool make good wooden puzzles and list suggested age groups on them. These suggested ages should be considered, but it is still good to know the abilities of the child you are buying for as he might be able to handle something more complex. The more experience the child has with puzzles, the more difficult ones he will be able to tackle. All puzzles list their total number of pieces, and many of the cardboard ones have a size sample printed on the box. This information can also indicate the

*A sampling of puzzles: front row, a 24-piece jigsaw puzzle featuring one of the* Sesame Street *characters; Rubik's Cube; 5-piece noninterlocking puzzles; middle row, 100-piece jigsaw puzzle; top row, 250-piece jigsaw puzzle; 500-piece jigsaw puzzle suitable for the whole family.*

suitability of a puzzle for a particular age group. The following guidelines are useful:

- *ages 6–18 months*—Fisher-Price's brightly colored, lightweight plastic three-piece crib and playpen puzzles are good choices
- *ages 2–3*—four- or five-piece wooden puzzles
- *ages 4–6*—fifteen or twenty-five to about fifty pieces (here we begin to move into cardboard jigsaw puzzles)
- *ages 6–8*—fifty to one hundred pieces
- *ages 8–10*—one hundred to five hundred pieces
- *age 10 to adult*—five hundred to two thousand pieces

The puzzles in the last category make an excellent family activity, which can be pursued intermittently but especially on those long winter evenings and weekends. Nothing is more pleasant than conversation over a bowl of fresh popcorn and a difficult puzzle. Since you cannot finish it in one sitting, you must be able to leave it intact so that it can be picked up again where you left off. There is a puzzle in some stage of completion at all times in our house. We have a piece of 2-by-4-foot particle board (a 4-by-6-foot board is good for a one- to two-thousand-piece puzzle), which can be picked up at most hardware or lumber supply stores. When we are finished for the evening, we carefully slide the board under a bed until the next time.

In addition to the puzzles made by Fisher-Price and Playskool, some very good ones of varying levels of complexity are available from Milton Bradley. Springbok offers beautiful puzzles that make you want to do nothing less than seal them with preservative glue when finished and hang them on the wall. You can also find reproductions of paintings by artists such as Dali and Chagall, available from Falcon.

Consider including one puzzle among the Christmas gifts and buying others intermittently throughout the year, depending on the interest of your child.

## *Games*

Board and table-top games are another type of toy that has been in existence since antiquity. (Electronic games are discussed separately at the end of this chapter.) Game boards with their many pieces have been discovered in ancient Egyptian tombs. These were probably intended only for adults; today, however, there are hundreds of games on the market for children as well as their parents.

Most games offer a measure of entertainment and diversion. They also provide mental stimulation from learning the rules, concentrating on the action, and, as the child gets older, from planning strategies and anticipating and counteracting those of his opponent. If it is not a solitary game, it helps in

*Playing with Lakeside's Booby Trap, a game that calls for eye-hand coordination and skills of balance.* Photo by Larry Mulvehill, courtesy Toy Manufacturers of America

social interaction with others and in the development of cooperative as well as competitive behavior.

As the child gets chances to both win and lose, he will gain confidence and learn good sportsmanship. This brings us to the important question of whether or not parents should let their children win initially. My feeling is *yes*, they should do so most of the time. If the game calls for any element of skill at all, it is going to be an unequal contest between child and adult or between young child and older sibling. If we want our children to grow up playing games, we must start them off winning, to let them gain confidence. Of course, if they win all of the time they will not learn how to lose gracefully. We don't want to wait until they are old enough to beat the socks off us all by themselves before we put our full energies into winning.

*For the Preschool Child (3–6 Years Old)*

Games for this age group should not have requirements for play that exceed the child's capabilities. This will more likely cause frustration and misuse of the game rather than present a challenge. If a parent plays with the child, however, some of the complicated skills can be circumvented. For example, a 5-year-old can get a lot of enjoyment out of playing Monopoly with a parent acting as banker. Some games, such as those listed below, require no reading by the young player.

> Chutes and Ladders (Milton Bradley. This is based on an East Indian game called Moksha-Patamu, reputed to be more than seven thousand years old, in which good and evil—the ladders and snakes—exist side by side. The same basic game has also been called Snakes and Ladders.)
> Goldilocks and the Three Bears (Selchow & Righter)
> Winnie the Pooh Game (Parker Brothers)
> Candyland (Milton Bradley)
> Gingerbread Man (Selchow & Righter)
> The Three Little Pigs (Selchow & Righter)
> Candyland Bingo (Milton Bradley)
> Scrabble Alphabet Game (Selchow & Righter)

Milton Bradley's Memory can also be played with the very young child. This involves matched pairs of pictures that are turned face down on the table. Each round, the players turn up two cards. When a player turns up a pair of the same objects, or turns up one whose mate had been turned up on a previous round, and he remembers its place, he gets the pair. At the end of the game, the player with the most pairs wins.

With the preschool child, you can begin playing this game by simply taking some of the pairs, turning them face up, and asking the child to choose the items that are alike. Or take two cards—sometimes showing the same objects and sometimes different ones—present the pair to the child, and ask him if they are alike (an important differentiation skill that is needed for reading). Then take a few pairs, turn them face down, and let the child begin the game without being overwhelmed by a multitude of cards. Gradually the number of cards used for play can be increased. This inexpensive game will help the young child develop concentration, memory, and reading readiness skills.

Games for this age group should have no small or sharp pieces, which can cause serious injuries if they are swallowed.

These games depend completely on chance to determine the winner. The random pick of the color card in Candyland and the chance spin of a number in Chutes and Ladders determine how many moves the player will make toward the goal. Even though there is the element of chance, the egocentric young child will often feel that he is somehow responsible for his progress because *he* twirls the spinner or chooses the card. This gives him some feeling of control over whether or not he wins. For the same reason, try to choose games that require the development of some skill by the players (for example, color matching in Candyland and counting in Chutes and Ladders); it is important that the child see a connection between his actions and the outcome of the game.

### *For the Older Child (6 Years and Up)*

By the time children are 6 years old we want to avoid giving them games that depend solely on random behavior or chance to determine the scores. Games for this age group should help the player develop skills such as problem solving, decisionmaking, or "putting himself in his opponent's place" in order to develop a competing or blocking strategy. They should be intellectually stimulating as well as enjoyable. It is always a good idea to note the manufacturer's suggested age recommendations. As the child moves into games for the 8-year-old and above, the entire family will be able to become involved in the activity.

## **The Ten Basic Categories of Games**

Games can essentially be grouped into ten different categories. Knowing something about each category will help us avoid duplication and choose games that will develop all kinds of abilities. For example, if we know that Numbers Up, Perfection, I Scream, and Superfection all involve getting game pieces in place while racing against the clock and a spring mechanism that causes the pieces to pop up, we need only buy one game from that group.

## *Race Games*

With this type of game, there is generally a finish line of some kind, and the players move along a path or through a maze to get to it. There may be roadblocks or penalties that send the players back; usually some chance occurrence will determine the number of moves they are able to make in one turn. Many race games are good for young children because they need only concentrate on one thing at a time—getting to the finish line. For the young child, there are:

Candyland (Milton Bradley)
Winnie the Pooh Game (Parker Brothers)
Chutes and Ladders (Milton Bradley)
The Three Little Pigs (Selchow & Righter)
Gingerbread Man (Selchow & Righter)
Goldilocks and the Three Bears (Selchow & Righter)
Cinderella (Cadaco)
Mother Goose (Cadaco)
Snow White and the Seven Dwarfs (Cadaco)
Push Over (Parker Brothers)
Strawberry Shortcake in Big Apple City (Parker Brothers)
Mousetrap (Hasbro)
Frog Hoppers (Hasbro; also includes color matching)

The following are suitable race games for the older child to the adult (reading skills are required for many of them):

backgammon
Parcheesi (Selchow & Righter)
Catfish Bend (Selchow & Righter)

Guinness Book of World Records Game (Parker Brothers)
The Christmas Game (Holiday Games)
Ten Commandments Game (Cadaco; helps in learning Biblical information)
Signs Up (Parker Brothers; helps in spelling)
Doubletrack (Milton Bradley)
Oh What a Mountain (Milton Bradley)
Bonkers (Parker Brothers)
Uncle Wiggly Game (Parker Brothers)
Ruff House (Parker Brothers)
Sorry (Parker Brothers)
Can't Stop (Parker Brothers)

### *Positional or Configurational Games*

With these, the player tries to get his pieces into a specified design. For the youngster, good choices in this category are:

bingo
ABC Lotto, Animal Lotto, Zoo Lotto (Edu Cards)
Picture Dominoes (Pressman)
Picture Triominoes (Pressman)
tic tac toe
Scrabble ABC (Selchow & Righter)
Cootie (Schaper)
Around the Clock Solitaire (Edu Cards)
Candyland Bingo (Milton Bradley)
Raggedy Ann and Andy (Milton Bradley; also a race game)
Ship Shape (Hasbro; also includes color and geometric-shape matching)
Put and Play Match a Shape (Western Publishing; also geometric-shape matching)
Puzzle Perfection (Lakeside; also color matching)

Flowers and Butterflies (Waddington; also number matching)
Gingerbread Man (Selchow & Righter; also a race game)

For the older child to adult:

Connect Four (Milton Bradley)
Over and Out (Gabriel; also helps memory skills)
Touche (Gabriel)
Tric-Trac (Milton Bradley)
Yahtzee, Triple Yahtzee, Jackpot Yahtzee, Challenge Yahtzee (Lowe)
Tic Tac Toe Times Ten (Selchow & Righter)
Backgammon for Juniors (Selchow & Righter)
Stackominoes (Pressman)
Take Five (Gabriel)
Rack-O (Milton Bradley)
Sudden Death (Gabriel)
Slide Five (Milton Bradley)
Concentration (Milton Bradley; also helps memory skills)

## *Word Games*

These are suitable for the older child who has some reading and spelling skills.

Lotto (Selchow & Righter)
Got a Minute (Selchow & Righter)
Scrabble, Scrabble Crossword for Juniors, Scrabble Sentence Game for Juniors, Scrabble Sentence Cube Game, Scrabble Crossword Dominoes (Selchow & Righter)
Scoring Anagrams (Selchow & Righter)
Boggle (Parker Brothers)
Perquackey (Lakeside)
Word Yahtzee (Lowe)
Razzle (Parker Brothers)

Power Play (LJN)
Hangman (Milton Bradley)
RSVP Three-Dimensional Crossword Game (Selchow & Righter)
Bali (Avalon Hill)
Word Power (Avalon Hill)
Probe (Parker Brothers)
Ad-Lib, Duplicate Ad-Lib (Milton Bradley)

## *War Games*

Players are pitted against each other in a war for territory (as in Chinese checkers), to dispose of an opponent (checkers), or to win a symbolic victory (chess). These are generally suitable for the older child as they call for both the development of a winning strategy and the blocking of an opponent's strategy.

Battleship (Milton Bradley)
checkers
chess
Chinese checkers
Blarf (Parker Brothers)
Othello (Gabriel)
Stratego (Milton Bradley)
Stay Alive (Milton Bradley)
Amoeba Wars (Avalon Hill)
The Generals Game (Ideal)
Tactics II (Avalon Hill)
Go (Avalon Hill)
Mancala (Milton Bradley; this game is estimated to be about seven thousand years old)

## *Card Games*

Again, these tend to be for the older child as a youngster does not have the dexterity in his fingers to hold the cards and manipulate them. Depending on the game, they help develop skills of memory, concentration, pattern discernment, and strategy.

>Old Maid (Milton Bradley and other manufacturers)
>Uno (International Games)
>Animal Rummy (Whitman)
>Michigan Rummy (Pressman)
>Royal Rummy (Whitman)
>Poker-Keeno (Cadaco)
>Tripoley (Cadaco)

## *Accumulation Games*

These call for the collection of game pieces of some kind. They help teach basic counting skills and recognition of masses. Games for the older child also involve developing strategy and blocking an opponent's strategy.

For the younger child:

>Critter in the Candy (Gabriel)
>Even Elephants Forget (Parker Brothers; also a race game)
>Memory, Memory: Fronts and Backs, Memory: Animal Families (Milton Bradley; all involve remembering the placement of matching pairs, and accumulating the largest number of pairs to win)
>HiHo Cherry-O (Whitman)
>Cootie (Schaper; also a configuration game)
>Put and Take (Schaper)
>Babes in Toyland (Selchow & Righter)

For the older child:

>Payday (Parker Brothers)
>Monopoly (Parker Brothers)
>Careers (Parker Brothers)

Trust Me (Parker Brothers)
Wizard's Quest (Avalon Hill)
Easy Money (Milton Bradley)
MacDonald's Farm Game (Selchow & Righter)
Stocks and Bonds (Avalon Hill)
Stock Market (Avalon Hill)
Venture (Avalon Hill)
Acquire (Avalon Hill)
The Collector (Avalon Hill)
The Game of Life (Milton Bradley)
Signs Up (Parker Brothers; also helps spelling skills)
Allowance (Milton Bradley)

The following are *anti*-accumulation games—the object is to get rid of the game pieces:

Go for Broke (Selchow & Righter)
The Mad Magazine Game (Parker Brothers)

## *Logic and Deduction Games*

Games in this category include those in which a crime is solved by the players (Clue, Whodunit) as well as games in which something such as a hidden color pattern must be logically deduced (Mastermind). Children who have developed the intellectual skills necessary to apply logic and problem solving will be able to enjoy these.

Clue (Parker Brothers)
Electronic Deduction (Ideal)
Whodunit (Selchow & Righter)
Point of Law (Avalon Hill)
Mastermind (Invicta)

## *Quiz/Information Games*

Generally these are for children with reading skills. However, for the younger child there are Milton Bradley's

Sesame Street and Light and Learn (which uses batteries).
For the older child:

    Facts in Five (Avalon Hill)
    Go to the Head of the Class (Milton Bradley)
    Ten Commandments Game (Cadaco)
    Game of the States (Milton Bradley)

## *Games with a Time Element*
Games of this type require the player to set up a number of items before time runs out and disrupts the play:

    Numbers Up (Milton Bradley)
    I Scream (Lakeside)
    Perfection (Lakeside)
    Superfection (Lakeside)

## *Games that Require Eye-Hand Coordination, Balance Skills*
The following games call for various types of eye-hand coordination:

    Jack Straws (Parker Brothers)
    jacks
    Pigs A Popping (Castle)
    Tiddlywinks (Pressman)
    Jumbo Tiddlywinks (Milton Bradley)
    Mr. Mouth (Tomy)
    Knots off the Wall (Knots Company)
    Basket Little Net (Cadaco)
    Smack It (Hasbro)
    Bribbit (Milton Bradley)
    Toss Across (Ideal)
    Flash (Ideal)
    Ring Toss (Milton Bradley)

These games call for balancing items in various ways while removing some:

Don't Break the Ice (Schaper)
Operation (Milton Bradley)
Booby Trap (Lakeside)
Toothache (Waddington)
My Dog Has Fleas (Ideal)
Jaws Game (Ideal)
Tip It (Ideal)

And finally, these games involve balancing items while adding on to the pile:

Don't Tip the Waiter (Colorforms)
Tummy Ache Game (Colorforms)
Pile On (Hasbro)
Alligator Game (Ideal)

Games can be either exciting or frustrating, depending on whether they are suited to the child's level of development, and whether they offer a new and interesting experience. The list of individual games that are available is virtually endless. However, if we know that many of them fall into the same basic categories, we will be able to choose among them more intelligently, and will eventually acquire a diverse selection of games that is stimulating and appropriate.

### *Electronic Games*

There is, as we have seen, a universality to children's play and toys that extends past cultural and historical boundaries. Children of many different times and cultures have shared in methods of play and certain types of toys: dolls, dollhouses and miniatures, war toys, games, balls, rattles, ride-on toys (Socrates is said to have romped with his children as they

*A selection of electronic games:* front row, *Atari's Superman, Adventure,* and *Maze Craze* cartridges; game instruction booklets; console and controls; middle row, *Texas Instruments' Speak and Spell; Atari's Keyboard Controller, Brain Games, Warlords,* and *Night Driver* cartridges, paddle wheels; *Milton Bradley's Comp IV;* top row, *Milton Bradley's Simon.*

played on a hobbyhorse), mechanical toys, and pull toys. The changes that have occurred have been largely in the methods of manufacturing and the materials from which toys are made. Plastic, vinyl, polyester, and rubber, which were unknown generations ago, are a very important part of modern-day toy making. Toys have also become much more accessible to the general public. Many middle-class children today have more playthings than some royal offspring of ancient times. The shift in manufacturing methods from handcrafted to machine-made, and the growth of the toy industry, have put toys within the reach of many more children. Still, until quite recently, the situation has been as Antonia Fraser describes it in *A History of*

*Toys* (1966): "It is a pleasant if sobering thought that there have been practically no fundamental changes in toys since the days of the Egyptians when all of the types of our modern toys are discernible."

Now the invention of the silicon microcomputer chip has changed all that, of course. This innovation, which led to the development of the hand-held computer game, portends a revolution in the world of toys and play for all future generations.

Many electronic games promote a number of important developmental skills. They give practice in eye-hand coordination; some help develop such intellectual skills as memory, decisionmaking, spelling, mathematics, and strategic thinking. Unfortunately, adults have no pleasant childhood memories to fall back on when choosing electronic toys. One important thing to consider is whether the scoring or other reward of the game depends on chance, or whether the player gets an opportunity to exercise some skill. Be sure to pay attention to the manufacturer's suggested age recommendations, as a too-complex game will be frustrating for the child. If possible, play the game in the store *before* you take it home.

The overwhelming array of today's electronic games can be cut down to manageable size if they are grouped into five broad categories. I do not feel that the first three—sports, target, and horoscope games—offer the player much besides eye-hand coordination and some social interaction. Games in the last two categories—deduction, memory, and strategy games and educational games—are much better buys. However, I have included listings of a few appropriate games in each category.

## *Sports*

The particular sport chosen depends only on the buyer's (or recipient's) preference—games ranging from baseball to golf to auto and horse racing are available.

- Mattel's Baseball II, Soccer II, Football II, Hockey

- Coleco's Head to Head Baseball, Electronic Quarterback
- Milton Bradley's Microvision Bowling
- U.S. Games' Trick Shot Basketball, Super Sports Four, Air Disc Hockey and Pinball
- Kenner's Grand Prix

## Target Games

The goal in these games is to strike objects such as submarines, meteors, ships, and so forth, or, in the case of Tomy's Pac Man, to gobble up all the objects in sight.

- Mattel's Catastrophe, Armor Battle, Space Alert
- Epoch's Galaxy II, Invader Game
- Milton Bradley's Electronic Battleship
- Tomy's Pac Man

## Horoscope Games

These give your horoscope, based on your birthdate. They also answer questions and make predictions regarding future dates. Because of their more sophisticated nature, they tend to be more enjoyable for adults than children in the long run. Games in this category include:

- Coleco's Zodiac
- Mattel's Horoscope Computer

## Deduction, Memory, and Strategy Games

These games begin to involve real intellectual skills. The player of deduction games must figure out a hidden word (Scrabble Sensor) or multiple-digit numbers (Electronic Mastermind). In memory games, the player must remember flashing colors and tones to repeat an ever-increasing pattern. Strategy games are much like their counterparts in board games.

- Deduction Games
    - Selchow & Righter's Scrabble Sensor
    - Ideal's Electronic Detective
    - Parker Brothers' Stop Thief and Merlin (Merlin also plays Tic Tac Toe, Music Machine, Echo, Black Jack 13, and Magic Square)
    - Milton Bradley's Comp IV
    - Invicta's Electronic Mastermind
- Memory Games
    - Milton Bradley's Simon and Double Simon
    - Encore's Mimic Me
- Strategy Games
    - Ideal's The Generals
    - Gabriel's Computer Othello
    - Sci Sys's Graduate Chess
    - Fidelity's Champion Sensory Chess Challenger

## Educational Games

- Math (quizzing players on addition, subtraction, multiplication, and division)
    - Texas Instruments' Speak and Math, Li'l Prof
    - Coleco's Li'l Genius
- Spelling
    - Texas Instruments' Speak and Spell and Spelling Bee (Speak and Spell is probably one of the electronic toys most in demand. It has a humanlike voice that gives instant praise when a word is spelled correctly. It features a vocabulary of more than 200 words, and also contains four other games, including a version of "Hangman" called Mystery Word.)
- General Information
    - Mattel's Discovery System
    - Coleco's Quiz Wiz

*Best Buys*

I feel that the following computer games are *very good buys*, especially for children, because of the skills that they help develop. They are also very interesting and challenging, and with each you get a number of different games for the money:

Mimic Me
Speak and Spell
Merlin

Adults may find these three games, and Quiz Wiz also, enjoyable as a family activity.

Few children in today's world miss exposure in one fashion or another to electronic toys. Since many are similar and all are relatively expensive, special care should be exercised in selecting the best one for your child. Obviously, those that tap the largest number of skills are the most desirable and usually the most interesting.

## Video Games

For the preadolescent and adolescent, the most popular computer video games seem to be Atari and Mattel's Intellivision, with Magnavox's Odyssey a distant third. Even though Intellivision's games have a more realistic and lifelike appearance, the clear leader in sales is the Atari. When some preadolescents were asked why they preferred the Atari, one frequently mentioned reason was the larger number of cartridges—Atari has forty-two. (The cartridges for the various sets are not interchangeable, although Sears does make a console that will take the Intellivision cartridges.)

Though most of the games involve shooting some alien object or some sports simulation, there are a few that are intellectually stimulating. Both Atari and Intellivision have math-skill cartridges. Atari has a chess cartridge, and something called Maze Craze, in which the player finds his way out of a maze (this is good for the preschool child as well). The Brain Games cartridge, in which the player has to detect subtle differences in one of the four figures flashed on the screen, is also a good concept. Whether interest in it can be sustained is another issue. At this point it is too early to give a definite yes or no. Atari also makes a cartridge entitled Basic Computer Programming, which is a useful skill for anyone today. Some experts are predicting that 80 to 90 percent of all homes will be equipped with computers by the end of the century.

Video games are coming under a good deal of criticism for their addictive qualities and for the fact that they foster dependence on the screen for entertainment and information. If they become more than occasional stimulating fun for your family—if they start to supersede other forms of play and learning—they have assumed too much importance in your life. We should all keep an open mind and a critical eye on video games in the future.

# 8
# Children's Books

In these days of saturation-level visual communication and entertainment, what is the best sequence for introducing our children to the world of books and fostering a love for them and for reading itself? Of course, the introduction should begin in infancy. A mother once asked a famous psychologist, "When should I begin reading to my child?" The psychologist asked, "How old is your child?" The woman answered, "Five." The psychologist then replied, "Oh my dear lady, you are five years too late."

## The Infant's First Books

We don't have to begin reading to our children the day they are born, but we should definitely begin during the first year of life. We can inaugurate the process by presenting the child with the soft cloth or linen books that we may remember from our own early childhood (see also page 29). These can be introduced at about 6 or 7 months, or whenever the baby can sit up and handle objects adequately. Soft cloth books are increasingly available and easier to find than they were a decade ago. The child cannot possibly poke or cut himself with a sharp edge, as he might with a hard-cover or paperback book. The books are also "mouthable," which is important because the infant will be chewing on them. Because the books are cloth (some with a rather slick finish, others a soft cotton), they are easily washed by machine or with a damp cloth. They are also very sturdy and do not tear as readily as paper books would.

As the infant gets older—close to 1 year of age—and is less likely to injure himself, we can introduce thick-paged cardboard books. These are almost impossible to tear and can stand up to the often rough treatment (such as banging, pounding, being thrown out of the playpen, etc.) that they will receive. Many of these books contain no words, only brightly colored pictures of toys, animals, or numbered objects that are or soon will be a part of the child's experience.

It is important to begin "reading time" during infancy. Sitting with the infant, holding the book, pointing to and naming the objects shown is an excellent way to start the bedtime story ritual. Actually, any time of the day or evening is suitable, but bedtime, when the child is squeaky clean and sweet smelling, has traditionally been the best. It is also a very effective way of helping the toddler wind down from high-spirited activity and acts as a pleasant prelude to sleep. Even on nights when you are unable to read to the child, you might encourage him to look at the books quietly in bed for a few minutes before he drops off to sleep.

By the time he enters the second year of life, every child should own *at least* one counting book and one abecedarium. Some of the thick-paged cardboard books are also counting books, so one such book might suffice. You might want to check out several abecedaria from the library before you decide to buy a particular one. The following are all excellent abecedaria; my personal favorites for the very young are those illustrated by Anno, Burningham, the Provensens, and Wildsmith.

Anno, Mitsumasa. *Anno's Alphabet*
Burningham, John. *John Burningham's ABC*
Duvoisin, Roger. *A for the Ark*

Greenaway, Kate. *A Apple Pie* (This will probably be available only through the library.)
Munari, Bruno. *Bruno Munari's ABC*
Provensen, Alice and Martin. *A Peaceable Kingdom: The Shaker Abecedarius*
Sendak, Maurice. *Alligators All Around*
Wildsmith, Brian. *Brian Wildsmith's ABC*

The last "must-purchase" book for late infancy is a large, substantial copy of "Mother Goose," as it will be read throughout childhood.

The exact origins of the title "Mother Goose," whether French, English, or German, are forever lost in antiquity. It is known that the term "Mother Goose" is over a thousand years old. The mother of Charlemagne was called "Bertha with the goose feet," because she had one foot that was larger than the other. She liked children and spent time telling them stories. It is said that she was the original Mother Goose.

In 1697 Charles Perrault, the famous French storyteller, published a book of ten fairy tales entitled *Contes de Ma Mère l'Oye*, or *Tales of My Mother Goose*.

The first time a book appeared with the title "Mother Goose," containing the short rhymes that one associates with the name, was in England in 1781. An edition of *Mother Goose's Melodies* was advertised by the John Newbery Publishing Company. These rhythmic verses had probably been passed down by word of mouth for many generations before they were formally written down and published.

There is evidence that at least some of the nursery rhymes did refer to real people or were originally penned as political satire for adults. Again, this is difficult to document conclusively. In any case, young children could not care less about the original meanings of the verses or for whom they were first intended. They love them for the pleasure they get from the pictures and the musical rhyming sounds of the verses. Nursery rhymes are often the child's first introduction to poetry, and the best editions of nursery rhymes also include outstanding artwork done specifically for children.

Nursery rhymes should be introduced, just as the name indicates, in the nursery. By the time the child is 2 or 3, he should have heard them so often that the first word or so will give him the cue to complete some of the verses. Some kindergarten teachers sadly report that today many children come to school never having heard a nursery rhyme. I hope that will soon be changing, as there seems to be a renewed interest in "Mother Goose" and her pleasant melodies.

Many nursery rhymes have all of the elements of a good novel, in very brief form, and are short enough for the toddler's attention span. For example, we encounter many characters who are children and who are within the experiential reach of the toddler, such as "Little Miss Muffett," "Lazy Little Boy Blue," "Sweet Tooth Jack-a-Dandy," the naughty little girl with a curl, and mischievous "Georgie Porgie." Plots with moral wrongs corrected occur in "The Queen of Hearts," "Tom, Tom, the Piper's Son," and "Ding Dong Bell." Sheer fantasy is expressed in "Old Mother Goose," "Hey Diddle Diddle," and "There Was an Old Woman Tossed in a Basket." Counting rhymes occur in such verses as "1, 2, Buckle My Shoe" and "1, 2, 3, 4, 5, I Caught a Fish Alive." For the riddle lover there are "As I Was Going to St. Ives," "Little Nancy Etticoat," and "Elizabeth, Elspeth, Betsy and Bess." Animals are mentioned in "Hickety, Pickety My Black Hen," "Baa, Baa, Black Sheep," "Mary Had a Little Lamb," "If Wishes Were Horses," "To Market, to Market, to Buy a Fat Pig," and "Pussy Cat, Pussy Cat, Where Have You Been?" Weather is covered in "Rain, Rain Go Away," "The North Wind Doth Blow," and "One Misty, Moisty Morning." (On rainy school mornings I often awaken my children with this verse to prepare them for the weather that awaits them.)

One of the following editions of "Mother Goose" will be returned to time and time again during the childhood years:

Caldecott, Randolph, ill. *Hey Diddle Diddle Picture*

*A selection of books for the young child:* Pattycake *(a soft cloth book);* Playdays *(thick-paged cardboard);* Dr. Seuss's A BC *(abecedarium);* Blanche Wright's The Real Mother Goose, Randolph Caldecott's Hey Diddle Diddle and Other Funny Poems *(nursery rhymes);* Mitsumasa Anno's Anno's Journey *(picture book);* Anno's The King's Flower, A Day at the Zoo *(replica of a Victorian pop-up book),* Maurice Sendak's Outside Over There, *and Donald Hall's* Oxcart Man, *1980 Caldecott Medal winner (picture storybooks).*

    Book. (This book is probably available only from the library but should be borrowed for its historical value.)

DeAngeli, Marguerite, ill. *Marguerite DeAngeli's Book of Nursery and Mother Goose Rhymes*

Emberley, Ed, ill. *London Bridge Is Falling Down: The Song and Game.* (Available only from the library.)

Galdone, Paul, ill. *The House that Jack Built*

Greenaway, Kate, ill. *Mother Goose.* (First published by G. Routledge, London, in 1881, and reissued by Crown Publishing in 1978. While this is an extremely important edition historically, the coloring in the reissued edition is a little too vivid, compared to the original, in my opinion. Kate Greenaway used delicate, muted pastels in her illustrations, and it seems as if, in order to keep the colors from washing out too much upon reproduction, they were brightened. A little of the delicacy is lost. However, if this does not bother you—and it probably won't if you have not seen the originals—in all other respects, this is an excellent edition.)

Hildebrandt, Tim and Greg, ills. *A Treasury of Best Loved Rhymes.* (This book is comprised of beautifully done multi-ethnic and multi-racial modern-day and period illustrations.)

Jeffers, Susan, ill. *If Wishes Were Horses.* (This book consists of eight beautifully illustrated nursery rhymes about horses.)

Richardson, Frederick, ill. *Mother Goose: The Classic Volland Edition.* (A must purchase!)

Scarry, Richard, ill. *Richard Scarry's Best Mother Goose Ever*

Sendak, Maurice, ill. *Hector Protector and As I Went over the Water*

Spier, Peter, ill. *London Bridge Is Falling Down*

Tripp, Wallace, ill. *Granfa' Grig Had a Pig and Other Rhymes without Reason from Mother Goose*

Wildsmith, Brian, ill. *Brian Wildsmith's Mother Goose*

Wright, Blanche, ill. *The Real Mother Goose.* (This book was originally published in 1916, but was reprinted as recently as 1978, so it should still be available.)

(Note: All the editions I've mentioned, except those by Caldecott and Emberley, should be available in bookstores. Children's librarians can easily direct you to other "Mother Goose" editions.)

Now that you have purchased an infant's library consisting of:

- soft cloth or linen books

- thick-paged cardboard books
- counting book
- abecedarium and
- "Mother Goose"

you can begin your children's book program—*at the library.* In these inflationary times, the children's room of your neighborhood library is the best book bargain going. We cannot afford to buy as many books as we can borrow from the library. Many times our family will leave the library with more than thirty books. Some nights we read five or six (many picture books take only a few minutes to read), and usually we have finished them all by the due date.

Managing that many books every month takes a bit of organization. First, every child should have a bookshelf in his room and be reminded to return the books to the shelf after he finishes reading them. Second, you should note the number of books that you get each time from the library—our family keeps track on a piece of paper held to the side of the refrigerator with a magnet. When we get ready to go to the library, the number of books we have in hand is checked against the number on the refrigerator to make sure that none is missing. It is amazing how having to spend a lot of time searching for a missing library book acts as a very strong incentive to put books back on the shelf after use. This is also an important lesson in the care and treatment of books.

Another good reason for borrowing books from the library rather than buying all of them is that children don't want to hear or read many books more than once. Buying such a limited-value book is a tremendous waste of money. I am reminded of the statement made by a true bibliophile of another time: "Some books are to be tasted, others leisurely chewed and others swallowed and digested." We should borrow from the library the books we want our children to taste; and *buy* the ones that our children want to swallow and digest.

Ask the children's librarian to recommend some good

books for beginners. He or she will be able to steer you to many excellent choices. Sometimes the library will have printed up a list of books for the young child, which will serve as a handy reference.

Trips to the children's room can be a totally absorbing and pleasurable experience. There will be not only books but, in many instances, toys and art reproductions that can be checked out as well.

### *Fostering a Love of Reading*

Studies have shown that children who begin to read as soon as possible maintain significant gains in verbal intelligence throughout the elementary school years. However, in this whole process of introducing books and reading, you must be aware of and respect the individual needs and timing of the child. You can nudge, but you cannot shove. You can encourage, but you must not force the issue. For example, nothing gave my firstborn greater pleasure than getting his bath, insisting that I get "nice and toasty warm under the cuthers" with him, and having story after story read aloud. Instead of cuddling a stuffed animal, he would go to sleep with a bed full of books. His love for reading still persists a decade later.

His little sister, however, was a different matter and could not be bothered with books. While being read to, she would yawn, stretch her arms over the page, and in numerous other ways show that she clearly was not interested. Even though I could not put out of my head terrible thoughts that we were on our way to having a nonreader, I left her alone. We still made our regular trips to the library, but she would spend most of the time playing with the toys and puzzles rather than books. It was not until she was almost 4 that she began to show an interest in books and express a consistent desire to be read to. Within a year's time, she was reading, and now at age 8, she is also very much a bibliophile. It was difficult, but I am glad that we did not force the issue and make reading a dreaded task instead of the joyous one it should be.

## *Picture Books*

As your child leaves infancy and you begin taking him regularly to the library (as regularly as your schedule can manage, even if it is only once a month), what types of books should you choose? Picture books are good to start with. In these, the illustrations are the primary focus. There are no words in the text, or very few words. There may or may not be a plot. The major pleasure comes from looking at the illustrations. The first picture book produced especially for children was published during the 1650s and was entitled *Orbis Pictus*. It was very formal, included a great deal of serious information, and probably would not be liked very much by today's young children.

Color picture books for children did not appear until the 1800s. The three nineteenth-century British illustrators who had the greatest impact on children's picture books were Walter Crane, Kate Greenaway, and Randolph Caldecott. While Crane's and Caldecott's work are not so easy to find in bookstores today, there have been recent reissues of Kate Greenaway's work. The library, however, should have books illustrated by Crane and Caldecott.

Examples of excellent recently published picture books include:

>Alexander, Martha. *Out, Out, Out*
>———. *Bobo's Dream*
>Anno, Mitsumasa. *Anno's Italy*
>———. *Anno's Journey*
>———. *Topsy Turvies*
>———. *Anno's Counting Book*
>———. *Anno's Britain*
>(There is so much going on within the oversize Anno

illustrations, so much detail and depth, that each page is a feast for the eyes. One of his books is a *must purchase*.)

Aruego, Jose, and Ariane Dewey. *We Hide, You Seek*
Ungerer, Tomi. *One, Two, Where's My Shoe?*
———. *Snail, Where Are You?*

(In *We Hide, You Seek*, animals illustrated in vivid tones are garbed in protective coloring. On one page, they are hiding and the child gets a chance to discover their hiding place; on the next page, they are coming out of hiding. Shoes and snails are hidden away in various pictures in the two Ungerer books. All of these books help the child to see a small hidden object that is part of a larger configuration, a very important cognitive ability. Not only is this exercise useful in sharpening visual skills and abstract divergent and convergent thinking, but it can also be applied in a very concrete way to seeing small words buried in larger configurations of letters after the child begins reading.)

Carle, Eric. *Do You Want to Be My Friend?*
———. *1, 2, 3, to the Zoo*
———. *I See a Song*
Emberley, Ed. *A Birthday Wish*
Wezel, Peter. *The Good Bird*
———. *The Bad Bird*
Wildsmith, Brian. *Brian Wildsmith's ABC*
———. *Brian Wildsmith's 1, 2, 3*

A second category of books is picture storybooks. These have great illustrations as well, but they also have text with characters and a plot. The pictures are an important and integral part of the story. And after a reading or two, the child is able to pick up the book, "read" the pictures, and give a surprisingly good rendition of the story, before he can actually discern the words.

## Caldecott Books

When choosing picture storybooks, we cannot go wrong with Caldecott Medal books or Caldecott Honor books.

The Caldecott Medal is awarded annually for the most distinguished American children's picture book. It was first awarded in 1938 and owes its existence to a man named Frederic Melcher, who was the editor of the *American Publisher's Weekly*. He named the award after Randolph Caldecott, who, as previously mentioned, along with Kate Greenaway and Walter Crane was one of the first illustrators to have a profound effect on children's books. (There is also a Greenaway Medal given for the best British children's picture book.) The winner of the Caldecott Medal is chosen by the Children's Services Division of the American Library Association. A book that wins the Caldecott Medal will have a round, gold-embossed Caldecott seal on its jacket. The Caldecott Honor books, which were runners-up for the Caldecott Medal, display a round silver-embossed seal. The Caldecott books are always a good purchase because the magnificent pictures almost guarantee that children will return to them often. Many of these books are available in the library, and some can still be found for purchase in various bookstores.

Following is a list of the Caldecott books, their authors, and the year in which they won the award:

| Year | Book Title | Author |
| --- | --- | --- |
| 1982 | *Jumanji* | Van Allsburg, Chris |
| 1981 | *Fables* | Lobel, Arthur |
| 1980 | *Ox-Cart Man* | Hall, Donald; Cooney, Barbara, ill. |
| 1979 | *Girl Who Loved Wild Horses* | Goble, Paul |
| 1978 | *Noah's Ark* | Spier, Peter |
| 1977 | *Ashanti to Zulu: African Traditions* | Musgrove, Margaret W.; Dillon, Leo and Diane, ills. |
| 1976 | *Why Mosquitoes Buzz in People's Ears* | Aardema, Verna; Dillon, Leo and Diane, ills. |
| 1975 | *Arrow to the Sun* | McDermott, Gerald |

(Caldecott Books continued)

| Year | Book Title | Author |
|---|---|---|
| 1974 | *Duffy and the Devil* | Zemach, Harve; Zemach, Margot, ill. |
| 1973 | *The Funny Little Woman* | Mosel, Arlene; Lent, Blair, ill. |
| 1972 | *One Fine Day* | Hogrogian, Nonny |
| 1971 | *A Story, a Story* | Haley, Gail |
| 1970 | *Sylvester and the Magic Pebble* | Steig, William |
| 1969 | *The Fool of the World and the Flying Ship* | Ransome, Arthur; Shulevitz, Uri, ill. |
| 1968 | *Drummer Hoff* | Emberley, Barbara; Emberley, Ed, ill. |
| 1967 | *Sam, Bangs, and Moonshine* | Ness, Evaline |
| 1966 | *Always Room for One More* | Nic Leodhas, Sorche; Hogrogian, Nonny, ill. |
| 1965 | *May I Bring a Friend?* | De Regniers, Beatrice S.; Montresor, Beni, ill. |
| 1964 | *Where the Wild Things Are* | Sendak, Maurice |
| 1963 | *The Snowy Day* | Keats, Ezra J. |
| 1962 | *Once a Mouse* | Brown, Marcia |
| 1961 | *Baboushka and the Three Kings* | Robbins, Ruth; Sidjakov, Nicolas, ill. |
| 1960 | *Nine Days to Christmas* | Ets, Marie H., and Labastida, Aurora; Ets, Marie H., ill. |
| 1959 | *Chanticleer and the Fox* | adapted from Chaucer; Cooney, Barbara, adaptor and ill. |
| 1958 | *Time of Wonder* | McCloskey, Robert |
| 1957 | *A Tree Is Nice* | Udry, Janice; Simont, Marc, ill. |
| 1956 | *Frog Went A-Courtin'* | Langstaff, John; Rojankovsky, Feodor, ill. |
| 1955 | *Cinderella* | Perrault, Charles; Brown, Marcia, ill. |
| 1954 | *Madeline's Rescue* | Bemelmans, Ludwig |
| 1953 | *The Biggest Bear* | Ward, Lynd |
| 1952 | *Finders Keepers* | Lipkind, William; Mordvinoff, Nicolas, ill. |
| 1951 | *The Egg Tree* | Milhous, Katherine |
| 1950 | *Song of the Swallows* | Politi, Leo |
| 1949 | *The Big Snow* | Hader, Berta and Elmer |
| 1948 | *White Snow, Bright Snow* | Tresselt, Alvin R.; Duvoisin, Roger, ill. |

| Year | Book Title | Author |
|------|------------|--------|
| 1947 | *The Little Island* | McDonald, Golden; Weisgard, Leonard, ill. |
| 1946 | *The Rooster Crows* | Petersham, Maud and Miska |
| 1945 | *Prayer for a Child* | Field, Rachel; Jones, Elizabeth Orton, ill. |
| 1944 | *Many Moons* | Thurber, James; Slobodkin, Louis, ill. |
| 1943 | *The Little House* | Burton, Virginia |
| 1942 | *Make Way for Ducklings* | McCloskey, Robert |
| 1941 | *They Were Strong and Good* | Lawson, Robert |
| 1940 | *Abraham Lincoln* | D'Aulaire, Ingri and Edgar |
| 1939 | *Mei Li* | Handforth, Thomas |
| 1938 | *Animals of the Bible* | Fish, Helen Dean; Lathrop, Dorothy, ill. |

Here is a partial list of Caldecott Honor books. Our family has read and enjoyed every one. These books should be available in libraries and some can still be found in bookstores.

| Book Title | Author |
|------------|--------|
| *Anansi the Spider: A Tale from the Ashanti People* | McDermott, Gerald |
| *Anatole* | Titus, Eve |
| *Anatole and the Cat* | Titus, Eve |
| *Bartholomew and the Oobleck* | Dr. Seuss |
| *Blueberries for Sal* | McCloskey, Robert |
| *Frederick* | Lionni, Leo |
| *Goggles* | Keats, Ezra J. |
| *Hide and Seek Fog* | Tresselt, Alvin |
| *The House that Jack Built* | Frasconi, Antonio |
| *If I Ran the Zoo* | Dr. Seuss |
| *In the Night Kitchen* | Sendak, Maurice |
| *Just Me* | Ets, Marie H. |
| *Little Bear's Visit* | Minarik, Else H. |
| *McElligot's Pool* | Dr. Seuss |
| *Mr. Rabbit and the Lovely Present* | Zolotow, Charlotte |
| *Moja Means One: The Swahili Counting Book* | Feelings, Muriel |
| *The Moon Jumpers* | Udry, Janice |
| *One Morning in Maine* | McCloskey, Robert |

*(Caldecott Honor Books continued)*

| Book Title | Author |
|---|---|
| *Play with Me* | Ets, Marie H. |
| *Stone Soup* | Brown, Marcia |
| *The Storm Book* | Zolotow, Charlotte |
| *Swimmy* | Lionni, Leo |
| *Umbrella* | Yashima, Taro |
| *What Do You Say, Dear?* | Joslin, Sesyle |
| *Why the Sun and Moon Live in the Sky* | Dayrell, Elphinstone |

It is important that young children be introduced to excellent artwork through the illustrations in their books. The bright primary colors and simple line drawings found in many books are fine and have their place in the child's literary diet. However, children will quickly learn to appreciate the softer, more subtle muted colors and greater complexity and depth found in the artwork of outstanding children's picture books. They should also get a chance to see various styles of illustrations. When we appreciate the time, consideration, intensity, and effort that great illustrators such as Barbara Cooney, Maurice Sendak, Robert McCloskey, and Mitsumasa Anno, among others, put into their work, we realize that every child should be able to experience their books.

As you begin to check out books regularly from the library, you will get a feeling for the kinds of books and particular authors and illustrators you and your children find enjoyable. Also be on the lookout for any new books done by an author/illustrator who has won the Caldecott Medal. Our family returns time and time again to the books of:

Mitsumasa Anno
Martha Alexander
Edward Ardizzone
Marcia Brown
John Burningham
Virginia Burton
Barbara Cooney
Ezra J. Keats
Leo Lionni
Robert McCloskey
Gerald McDermott
Beatrix Potter
Eleanor Schick
Maurice Sendak

Roger Duvoisin
Ed Emberley
Marjorie Flack
Kate Greenaway

Dr. Seuss
Peter Spier
Brian Wildsmith
Taro Yashima

Surprisingly, some of these excellent illustrators have not won the Caldecott award.

## *Storybooks*

In addition to a slight preference for color illustrations (although they also enjoy black and white), what are some of the other qualities that young children like in their stories? They like the rhythm and repetition in cumulative stories such as *The Three Little Pigs*, *The Little Red Hen*, *The Three Billy Goats Gruff*, and *The House that Jack Built*.

Children like hearing stories that their parents have had read to them. It fosters a sense of tradition. They also enjoy stories about animals, many of which will possess all the human characteristics, both positive and negative, and will get involved in some very human predicaments. Books of this type include:

Bond, Michael. *The Paddington Series*
De Brunhoff, Jean. *The Babar Series*
Hoban, Russell. *The Frances Series*
Leaf, Munro. *Ferdinand the Bull*
Minarik, Else. *The Little Bear Series*
Steig, William. *Sylvester and the Magic Pebble*
*The Three Billy Goats Gruff*
*The Three Little Pigs*
*The Three Bears*

For older readers, there are:

Grahame, Kenneth. *The Wind in the Willows*
Kipling, Rudyard. *Just So Stories*

Lawson, Robert. *Rabbit Hill*
Sewell, Anna. *Black Beauty*
White, E. B. *Charlotte's Web*

The other type of animal tale is the realistic one. Here the animal's behavior is true to its species. Most frequently, the animals are pets and the story is told from the point of view of the human owner. If, however, the story is from the perspective of the animal, he will behave in a typical animalistic way and will not speak. Books of this type for young readers are, for example, the *Angus* series by Marjorie Flack.

Older readers should enjoy:

Armstrong, William. *Sounder*
Henry, Marguerite. *King of the Wind*
———. *Misty of Chincoteague*
———. *Sea Star: Orphan of Chincoteague*
Knight, Eric. *Lassie Come Home*
Rawlings, Marjorie Kinnan. *The Yearling*

Stories that deal with children's particular interests and problems are especially enjoyed in picture storybooks. The reader rejoices when the character develops a new skill, one that he himself may be trying to master. Suggestions in this category include:

Brown, Myra Berry. *Sandy Signs His Name*
Flack, Marjorie. *Wait for William (To Tie His Shoes)*
Keats, Ezra J. *Whistle for Willie*

Discussions about experiences that the child may find anxiety producing may be facilitated by a story dealing with the same event. Separation, whether it is from the death of a loved one, the first day away from mom or dad at school, the loss of a friend, or being lost from one's mother or hospitalized, can be traumatic for the child. Yet in many instances, he cannot talk about his feelings. He may find it easier to verbalize his fears when he realizes that someone else (even a fictional character) has had the same problem.

Separation from the parent to attend school is dealt with in these books:

> Brienberg, Petronella. *Shawn Goes to School*
> Cohen, Miriam. *The New Teacher*
> Mannheim, Grete. *The Two Friends*
> Steiner, Charlotte. *I'd Rather Stay with You*
> Yashima, Taro. *Umbrella*

William Steig's *Sylvester and the Magic Pebble* also deals with separation from parents. Separation of friends occurs in Steig's *Amos and Boris* and in Else Minarik's *Little Bear's Friend*. The temporary loss of mother is dealt with in Robert McCloskey's *Blueberries for Sal*. Separation through death is the theme of Tomie DePaola's *Nana Upstairs and Nana Downstairs*. Separation through hospitalization occurs in Ludwig Bemelmans' *Madeline*, H. A. Rey's *Curious George Goes to the Hospital*, and Marjorie Sharmat's *I Want Mama* (in this the mother is hospitalized).

Bedtime fears and anxieties may be allayed somewhat from discussions that occur after reading the following:

> Beckman, Kaj. *Lisa Cannot Sleep* (You will probably have to get this excellent little story from the library as it is out of print.)
> Brown, Margaret W. *Goodnight Moon*
> Brown, Myra. *Benjy's Blanket*
> Hoban, Russell. *Bedtime for Frances*
> Dr. Seuss. *The Sleep Book*
> Waber, Bernard. *Ira Sleeps Over*

Emotional feelings such as anger, resentment, and pain are explored in books concerning the birth of a sibling, divorce, and other stressful situations. Again, the reading of one of these stories to the child at a critical time may serve as

an effective springboard to get him talking about his emotions.
Feelings of anger and resentment are treated in:

>Sendak, Maurice. *Where the Wild Things Are*
>Simon, Norma. *I Was So Mad!*
>Viorst, Judith. *Alexander and the Terrible, Horrible, No Good, Very Bad Day*
>Zolotow, Charlotte. *The Hating Book*
>———. *If It Weren't for You*

Painful feelings the child may experience as a result of parents divorcing or separating, or living in a one-parent family, are covered in:

>Simon, Norma. *I'm Busy Too*
>———. *All Kinds of Families*
>Stanek, Muriel. *I Won't Go Without a Father*
>Zolotow, Charlotte. *A Father Like That*

Various types of family groups are portrayed as coping very well in these books.

The feelings an older child may experience when a sibling arrives are the theme of:

>Alexander, Martha. *Nobody Asked Me If I Wanted a Baby Sister*
>———. *When the New Baby Comes, I'm Moving Out*
>Keats, Ezra J. *Peter's Chair*
>Schick, Eleanor. *Peggy's New Brother*

Young children at least 4 to 6 years old appreciate and enjoy subtlety in their stories. One is amazed at the degree of understanding they exhibit with regard to very subtle ideas expressed in children's literature. For example, children almost intuitively understand that the wife in the fable of *The Fisherman and His Wife*, who keeps prodding her husband to use his wishes to get greater and greater possessions, is very greedy.

The lesson needn't be repeated over and over again for them to get the idea, and it is more powerful if they are given the chance to realize it on their own.

Some excellent picture books of folktales from various cultures have been produced for young children. Not only will the children see some of the differences in times and cultures, but they will learn that there are universal truths. When the child is about 5 or 6 years old, we should start discussing the stories we read and asking questions. This is especially important with books that tap specific emotions and/or problems that the child might be experiencing, and with the fables and folktales that speak on two levels, the narrative and the underlying universal truth. This is good practice for developing the critical skills necessary in reading, discussing, and evaluating literature.

The following are some excellent picture-book fables and folktales for young children:

> Aardema, Verna. *Who's in Rabbit's House?*
> ———. *Why Mosquitos Buzz in People's Ears*
> Brown, Marcia. *Once a Mouse*
> Gobhai, Mehlli. *Usha, the Mouse Maiden*
> Haley, Gail. *A Story, a Story*
> McDermott, Gerald. *Arrow to the Sun*
> Scarry, Richard. *The Fables of LaFontaine*
> Wildsmith, Brian, ill. *The Hare and the Tortoise*
> ———. *The Lion and the Rat*
> ———. *The Miller, the Boy, and the Donkey*
> ———. *The North Wind and the Sun*
> ———. *The Rich Man and the Shoemaker*

As the child gains sufficient skills to begin to read on his own, look for books that are labeled "Easy to Read." Some of the Dr. Seuss books such as *Hop on Pop* and *Green Eggs and Ham* have a great deal of useful repetition of the same simple words. Also consult the children's librarian. Sometimes the library will have compiled a list of books for intermediate readers or young readers. This can be a valuable starting place. Then as the child begins to choose his own books, he will get a feeling for what it is he likes and will know where in the children's room of the library they can be found. As he leaves the "Easy to Read" books, he is ready to move into illustrated storybooks. These contain pictures, typically black and white, but they are relatively few and serve as a supplement to the text rather than as the primary focus of the book.

## *Books for Late Childhood and Adolescence*

The child of this age group—age 7 and beyond—will most likely begin with modern fiction about present-day characters. However, if he gets stuck in a "reading rut," we can provide some gentle nudging and guidance to get him to explore various other areas. Parents should be aware of what is available in various genres of literature so that they can guide the child into balanced reading.

Historical fiction is a logical and easy transition from modern fiction. One of the most important requirements of historical fiction is that the prevailing customs, behaviors, and situations of the era all be accurately represented. This kind of fiction is especially suitable for late childhood into adolescence, when the child is able intellectually to understand the concept of historical time. (Young children get some vague notions of "different" when they see the clothing and scenes in nursery rhymes and picture books, but they cannot understand these factors within the framework of linear time. They have more than they can handle trying to understand how many more days there are until Christmas.) Well-documented, well-written historical fiction, which does not always have to center around a particular historical event, allows the child a glimpse of another time and place.

For example, my oldest child once read to me a list of items served for breakfast in Laura Ingalls Wilder's *Farmer Boy*. The breakfast was of much greater quantity and diversity than those we eat today, and even included apple pie. This led to a discussion of the changing eating habits, the factors that necessitated that kind of heavy early-morning eating, and the increasing use of sugar today.

Examples of excellent historical fiction include:

Alcott, Louisa May. *The Little Women Series*
Brink, Carol Ryie. *Caddie Woodlawn*
Caudill, Rebecca. *Tree of Freedom*
De Angeli, Marguerite. *The Door in the Wall*
de Trevino, Elizabeth. *I, Juan de Pareja*
Edmonds, Walter. *The Matchlock Gun*
Estes, Eleanor. *The Moffat Series*
Field, Rachel. *Calico Bush*
Forbes, Esther. *Johnny Tremain*
Keith, Harold. *Rifles for Watie*
Kelly, Eric. *The Trumpeter of Krakow*
Lenski, Lois. *Indian Captive*
Lewis, Elizabeth. *Young Fu of the Upper Yangtze*
Marriott, Alice. *Indian Annie: Kiowa Captive*
O'Dell, Scott. *Island of the Blue Dolphins*
Polland, Madeleine. *To Tell My People*
Warner, Gertrude C. *The Boxcar Children*
Wilder, Laura I. *The Little House Series*

Biographies make the transition from fiction rather easy, as many biographies read like good novels. In addition to such classic biographies as those of Abraham Lincoln and George Washington, there are literally hundreds of others to be explored. Going through the biography shelves in the library, the child is bound to come upon a person in whom he is interested. One mother reported that for a couple of years her eldest chose only fiction and did not seem interested in anything else. After much nudging, he was finally persuaded to read some biographies. Now he reads fiction, biographies, jokes, tall tales, nonsense riddles, and fairy tales. He is also voraciously reading books about medical history and significant persons in the field of medicine.

*More books for the child's library:* Maurice Sendak's Nutshell Library, Richard Scarry's Cars and Trucks and Things That Go *(picture storybooks for early reading);* Madeleine L'Engle's A Wrinkle in Time *(Newbery Award winner);* Laura Ingalls Wilder's The First Four Years, Kenneth Grahame's The Wind in the Willows *(illustrated books for more advanced readers);* Grimm's Fairy Tales, Perrault's Classic French Fairy Tales, D'Aulaires' Book of Greek Myths *(fables and fairy tales).*

Nothing is more exhilarating than finding a book that you read as a child, introducing your children to it, and having them enjoy it also. Discuss the various books that you have both read. This gives the children experience in narration and in picking out the main ideas, in developing verbal fluency, in sequencing, and in summarizing.

With regard to recommending books, turn-about is also fair play. My 12-year-old has recommended several of his books to me. I have dutifully read them, and we have discussed them. Many times I will ask him to tell me about a book that he has read which I will not have the time to read. This pleases him exceedingly, and as a result, he is developing into a more than adequate storyteller.

## Newbery Medal Winners

Another good starting point for recommended reading is a list of the Newbery books. Again, the children's librarian can probably provide this list. The Newbery award is given annually to the author of the best children's book published during the previous year. Like the Caldecott Medal, the Newbery was conceived by Frederic Melcher, and was in fact started several years earlier than the Caldecott. The award is named after John Newbery, a writer and the first English children's book publisher. In 1744 Newbery published *A Little Pretty Pocket Book Intended for the Instruction and Amusement of Little Master Tommy and Pretty Miss Polly*; this book marked a significant milestone in children's literature, because it was primarily intended for diversion and entertainment rather than the teaching of strict moralistic lessons. Later he brought out a short novel specifically for children entitled *The Renowned History of Little Goody Two Shoes, Otherwise Called Mrs. Margery Two Shoes*.

The Newbery Medal winner is chosen by the Children's Services Division of the American Library Association. Here is a list of the Newbery winners, the year of their award, and their authors:

| Year | Book Title | Author |
|---|---|---|
| 1982 | *A Visit to William Blake's Inn: Poems for Innocent and Experienced Travelers* | Willard, Nancy |
| 1981 | *Jacob Have I Loved* | Paterson, Katherine |
| 1980 | *A Gathering of Days* | Blos, Joan |
| 1979 | *The Westing Game* | Raskin, Ellen |
| 1978 | *Bridge to Terabithia* | Paterson, Katherine |
| 1977 | *Roll of Thunder, Hear My Cry* | Taylor, Mildred |
| 1976 | *The Grey King* | Cooper, Susan |
| 1975 | *M. C. Higgins the Great* | Hamilton, Virginia |
| 1974 | *The Slave Dancer* | Fox, Paula |
| 1973 | *Julie of the Wolves* | George, Jean |
| 1972 | *Mrs. Frisby and the Rats of Nimh* | O'Brien, Robert |
| 1971 | *The Summer of the Swans* | Byars, Betsy |

(*Newbery Medal Winners continued*)

| Year | Book Title | Author |
|---|---|---|
| 1970 | *Sounder* | Armstrong, William |
| 1969 | *The High King* | Alexander, Lloyd |
| 1968 | *From the Mixed-Up Files of Mrs. Basil E. Frankweiler* | Konigsburg, E. L. |
| 1967 | *Up a Road Slowly* | Hunt, Irene |
| 1966 | *I, Juan de Pareja* | de Trevino, Elizabeth B. |
| 1965 | *Shadow of a Bull* | Wojciechowska, Maia |
| 1964 | *It's Like This, Cat* | Neville, Emily C. |
| 1963 | *A Wrinkle in Time* | L'Engle, Madeleine |
| 1962 | *The Bronze Bow* | Speare, Elizabeth |
| 1961 | *Island of The Blue Dolphins* | O'Dell, Scott |
| 1960 | *Onion John* | Krumgold, Joseph |
| 1959 | *The Witch of Blackbird Pond* | Speare, Elizabeth |
| 1958 | *Rifles for Watie* | Keith, Harold |
| 1957 | *Miracles on Maple Hill* | Sorensen, Virginia |
| 1956 | *Carry on, Mr. Bowditch* | Latham, Jean L. |
| 1955 | *The Wheel on the School* | De Jong, Meindert |
| 1954 | *And Now Miguel* | Krumgold, Joseph |
| 1953 | *Secret of the Andes* | Clark, Ann N. |
| 1952 | *Ginger Pye* | Estes, Eleanor |
| 1951 | *Amos Fortune, Free Man* | Yates, Elizabeth |
| 1950 | *The Door in the Wall* | De Angeli, Marguerite |
| 1949 | *King of the Wind* | Henry, Marguerite |
| 1948 | *The Twenty-One Balloons* | DuBois, William Pene |
| 1947 | *Miss Hickory* | Bailey, Carolyn S. |
| 1946 | *Strawberry Girl* | Lenski, Lois |
| 1945 | *Rabbit Hill* | Lawson, Robert |
| 1944 | *Johnny Tremain* | Forbes, Esther |
| 1943 | *Adam of the Road* | Gray, Elizabeth J. |
| 1942 | *The Matchlock Gun* | Edmonds, Walter |
| 1941 | *Call It Courage* | Sperry, Armstrong |
| 1940 | *Daniel Boone* | Daugherty, James |
| 1939 | *Thimble Summer* | Enright, Elizabeth |
| 1938 | *The White Stag* | Seredy, Kate |
| 1937 | *Roller Skates* | Sawyer, Ruth |
| 1936 | *Caddie Woodlawn* | Brink, Carol |
| 1935 | *Dobry* | Shannon, Monica |
| 1934 | *Invincible Louisa* | Meigs, Cornelia |
| 1933 | *Young Fu of the Upper Yangtze* | Lewis, Elizabeth F. |
| 1932 | *Waterless Mountain* | Armer, Laura A. |
| 1931 | *The Cat Who Went to Heaven* | Coatsworth, Elizabeth |

| Year | Book Title | Author |
|---|---|---|
| 1930 | *Hitty: Her First Hundred Years* | Field, Rachel |
| 1929 | *The Trumpeter of Krakkow* | Kelly, Eric |
| 1928 | *Gay-Neck: The Story of a Pigeon* | Mukerji, Dhan G. |
| 1927 | *Smoky, the Cowhorse* | James, Will |
| 1926 | *Shen of the Sea* | Chrisman, Arthur B. |
| 1925 | *Tales from Silver Lands* | Finger, Charles |
| 1924 | *The Dark Frigate* | Hawes, Charles |
| 1923 | *The Voyages of Doctor Dolittle* | Lofting, Hugh |
| 1922 | *The Story of Mankind* | Van Loon, Hendrik W. |

## *The Fairy Tale*

A final category that I feel is a much-neglected but very important one in children's literature is the fairy tale. Most young children do hear the picture storybook fairy tales of *The Three Little Pigs, Cinderella,* and *The Three Bears.* However, many never actually read illustrated books of fairy tales. My personal feeling is that many of the fairy tales can be frightening to a very young child, and that they should be read primarily during late childhood and early adolescence. For those who are concerned about the violence in fairy tales, it must be said that such violence is really controlled to some degree by the imagination of the reader. It does not begin to compare with the graphic violence visually portrayed on prime-time television. Also, none of the violence in fairy tales is senseless or wanton. Many times the malicious behavior that occurs in a fairy tale (such as a prince or princess being put under a spell) is reversible if some specific requirement is met (such as a kiss). The hero or heroine always manages to meet and surmount the difficult challenges, most often by using his or her own abilities. The guilty are punished and the punishment is never more severe than the crime.

After reading Dr. Bruno Bettelheim's book *The Uses of Enchantment,* I am convinced that fairy tales—which have been in all cultures at all times—speak to the child on many levels, teaching him that struggle, as Bettelheim puts it, "is an intrinsic part of human existence—but that if one does not shy away, but steadfastly meets unexpected and often unjust hardships, one masters all obstacles and at the end emerges victorious." While you may not agree with all of Dr. Bettelheim's psychoanalytic symbolism and interpretation of fairy tales, it is almost certain that you will come away from reading his book with an awareness of how very important it is that children be encouraged to read and enjoy fairy tales.

The following are good books of fairy tales:

> Aardema, Verna. *Tales for the Third Ear: From Equatorial Africa*
> Babbitt, Ellen. *The Jataka Tales*
> Brown, Marcia, ill. *Cinderella, or the Little Glass Slipper*
> ———. *Dick Whittington and His Cat*
> Grimm, Jacob and Wilhelm. *Grimm's Fairy Tales*
> Jacobs, Joseph, ed. *English Fairy Tales*
> ———. *The Pied Piper and Other Tales*
> Perrault, Charles. *Perrault's Fairy Tales*
> Sendak, Maurice, ill. *The Juniper Tree and Other Tales from Grimm*

## A Core Reading List for Young Children

The following reading list is meant to be a starting point for the well-read toddler, preschooler, kindergartener. There is no way to include all of the very good books that are available. Everyone who reads this will undoubtedly say, "You could have included. . . ." My only response to that is you're right, and add anything to the list that you like. This is just the beginning.

> Aardema, Verna. *Who's in Rabbit's House?*
> Alexander, Martha. *I'll Be the Horse if You'll Play with Me*
> ———. *Out, Out, Out*

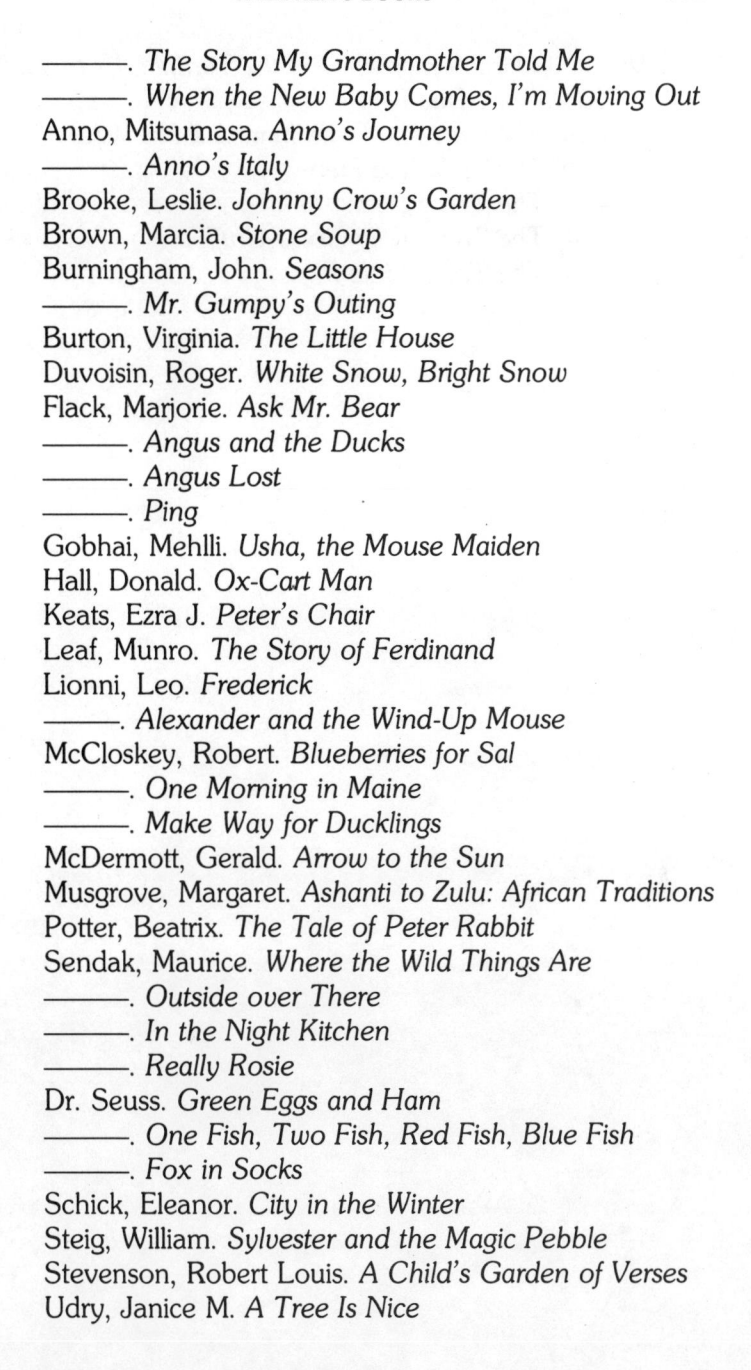

———. *The Story My Grandmother Told Me*
———. *When the New Baby Comes, I'm Moving Out*
Anno, Mitsumasa. *Anno's Journey*
———. *Anno's Italy*
Brooke, Leslie. *Johnny Crow's Garden*
Brown, Marcia. *Stone Soup*
Burningham, John. *Seasons*
———. *Mr. Gumpy's Outing*
Burton, Virginia. *The Little House*
Duvoisin, Roger. *White Snow, Bright Snow*
Flack, Marjorie. *Ask Mr. Bear*
———. *Angus and the Ducks*
———. *Angus Lost*
———. *Ping*
Gobhai, Mehlli. *Usha, the Mouse Maiden*
Hall, Donald. *Ox-Cart Man*
Keats, Ezra J. *Peter's Chair*
Leaf, Munro. *The Story of Ferdinand*
Lionni, Leo. *Frederick*
———. *Alexander and the Wind-Up Mouse*
McCloskey, Robert. *Blueberries for Sal*
———. *One Morning in Maine*
———. *Make Way for Ducklings*
McDermott, Gerald. *Arrow to the Sun*
Musgrove, Margaret. *Ashanti to Zulu: African Traditions*
Potter, Beatrix. *The Tale of Peter Rabbit*
Sendak, Maurice. *Where the Wild Things Are*
———. *Outside over There*
———. *In the Night Kitchen*
———. *Really Rosie*
Dr. Seuss. *Green Eggs and Ham*
———. *One Fish, Two Fish, Red Fish, Blue Fish*
———. *Fox in Socks*
Schick, Eleanor. *City in the Winter*
Steig, William. *Sylvester and the Magic Pebble*
Stevenson, Robert Louis. *A Child's Garden of Verses*
Udry, Janice M. *A Tree Is Nice*

Viorst, Judith. *Alexander and the Terrible, Horrible, No Good, Very Bad Day*
(various authors.) *The Fisherman and His Wife*
———. *The Little Red Hen*
———. *The Three Bears*
———. *The Three Billy Goats Gruff*
———. *The Three Little Pigs*

# 9
# Toys for Children with Special Needs

## The Gifted Child

According to the Office of the Gifted and Talented, which was established within the U.S. Office of Education in 1972, gifted children are those who are "capable of high performance, including those with demonstrated achievement or ability in any one or more of these areas—general intellectual ability, specific academic aptitude, creative or productive thinking, leadership ability, visual and performing arts or psychomotor ability." It is estimated that approximately 3 to 5 percent of the school-age population—some two to five million children—could be considered especially talented and gifted.

There are certain characteristics that tend to be associated with the gifted, and parents should be aware of them as many children demonstrate evidence of giftedness before they enter school:

1. The gifted child may walk and talk earlier than his peers. His vocabulary may be much larger and his use of language more advanced than that of other children his age.
2. The gifted child may begin reading early, often

before age 4. Sometimes he will have learned to read almost by himself.
3. Curiosity—asking a lot of questions, always wondering why—is another typical characteristic of the gifted.
4. The gifted child may demonstrate high powers of concentration. He may become so deeply engrossed in an activity that he is unaware of things going on around him.
5. His interests become wide-ranging and may shift frequently. One month he might want to know about whales; the next, his interest may lie in mythology.
6. He is imaginative, able to think abstractly and understand complex concepts that may be out of the reach of other children his age. He may also perceive relationships in objects or situations that elude other children. For example, one gifted youngster announced that "The Bear Went over the Mountain," "For He's a Jolly Good Fellow," and his soccer team's theme song all had the same melody.
7. They tend to have a well-developed sense of humor, which may be demonstrated at an early age.
8. They may demonstrate creative abilities in writing, art, and so on, as well as an interest in numbers and puzzles early on.
9. They tend to set very high standards for themselves, and judge themselves much more stringently than others would.
10. Their thinking tends to be fluid, flexible, and original in many instances.
11. They may enjoy the company of adults—parents, adult acquaintances, and teachers—more than they do their peers. Often they can carry on stimulating conversations with adults.
12. They often exhibit a highly developed moral and ethical sense and will stick to their ideas even if it means nonconformity with their peers. Sometimes

the gifted child will have problems in the social area with his peers.
13. Though they may have a well-defined and highly valued sense of self, they may hide their abilities in order not to appear different from their peers, especially if they have been ostracized for their giftedness.

Of course, in infancy these characteristics will not yet be demonstrated. However, if parents provide the type of toys and stimulation called for in chapter 2, the gifted youngster will not have been shortchanged. As he moves into early childhood, parents would do well to follow the child's lead and provide toys and activities that feed his particular interests. He may show above-average abilities in one area and not in another.

One thing to keep in mind is that the gifted child is, first of all, a child. While we want him to use his intellectual gifts and play with toys that stimulate him mentally, we by no means want to overlook the areas of social, physical, and creative development. The first toys for these other developmental areas should be the same as those for any other child. As the gifted child develops, the following additional playthings may be of interest to him:

*Puzzles and Brainteasers*

*Mathematical Puzzles for Beginners and Enthusiasts* by Geoffrey Mott-Smith (Dover Publications)
*Math Puzzles and Games* by Michael Holt (Walker and Company)
*Perplexing Puzzles and Tantalizing Teasers* by Martin Gardner (Archway)
*Fun with Words* by Maxwell Nurnberg (Prentice-Hall)
*The Mammoth Book of Word Games* by Richard Manchester (Hart Publishing Company)

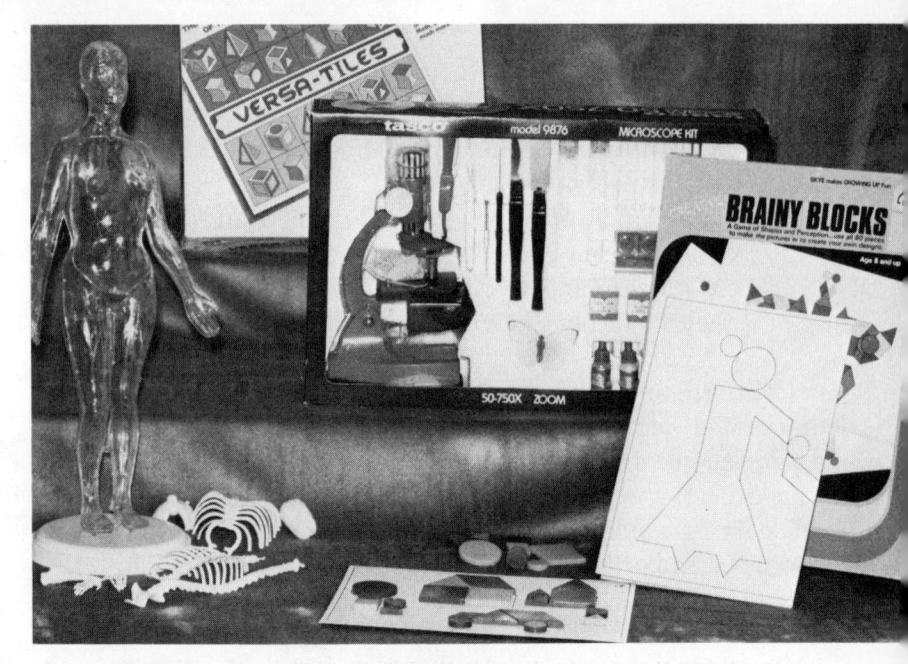

*Some toys for the gifted child:* front row, *Revell's Visible Woman; Sky's Brainy Blocks (teach spatial relationships);* middle row, *Tasco's Microscope Kit;* top row, *American Testing Association's Versa-Tiles (matching and logic cards).*

*Games*

>American Testing Association's Versa-Tiles (matching colors, shapes)
>Avalon Hill's Risk, Sleuth, Acquire, Stocks and Bonds, Venture, Facts in Five
>Selchow & Righter's Scrabble
>Lakeside's Perquackey
>chess

*Creative, Constructive Activities and Hobbies*

>calligraphy kit
>bookbinding kit
>lithography kit
>sketching pads, drawing materials

# TOYS FOR CHILDREN WITH SPECIAL NEEDS

painting, sculpting supplies
*Altair Design* (a book by Ensor Holiday, published by Pantheon. Geometric shapes are colored in to make an infinite variety of pictures; suitable for a wide age stamp or coin collection group)
Brainy Blocks (Skye; use different shapes to create pictures, learn spatial relationships)
Motorized Tinkertoys (Gabriel)
moving vehicle construction sets (Fisher Technics)
model car, boat, airplane kits
dinosaur skeleton assembly kit
notebooks for writing observations, keeping a journal, etc.

*For Exploring, Examining, Experimenting*

globe
microscope
magnifying glass
binoculars
telescope
chemistry set
Visible Man (Electrolab), Visible Woman (Scientifics Kit)
stethoscope
ant farm
silk factory (watching silkworms spin)
aquarium
terrarium
rock polishing kit

See also pages 56–58 for more suggestions.

*Books*

See chapter 8 for detailed suggestions. Also, a good set of home encyclopedias would be a sound investment. As one gifted child was overheard to say to a guest, "Let's go look at some encyclopedias, that's fun." (One can only imagine what the guest thought of the suggestion.)

Many gifted children are fascinated by words, so the following reference books might be purchased along with the standard dictionary: a rhyming dictionary, thesaurus, books on etymology.

### *The Blind or Visually Handicapped Child*

The first toys for the blind infant should be ones that stimulate the senses rather than ones that must be handled. Even though immediately after birth the visually handicapped infant does not have the muscular control necessary to voluntarily grasp a toy and is lacking his sense of vision, he does have at his disposal the remaining senses, which are already functioning in a somewhat limited fashion. He uses the available sensory channels to begin to learn about and organize his environment, to become aware of himself as a discrete and separate entity, and to discover the significant others in his life. (For a more complete discussion of the sensory capabilities present at birth or shortly thereafter, see chapter 3.)

The most important sensory channel to the blind infant's external environment is his hearing. Therefore, rich, varied auditory stimulation is vital from birth onward. The human voice, very important for all infants, becomes even more so for the blind, and he should be talked to, crooned to, and sung to from the first day of birth.

Toys that provide auditory stimulation can be used as soon as the infant is in the crib. The sound of the mother's heartbeat and the movement of the amniotic fluid are reproduced in Rushton's Rock-A-Bye Bear. When the bear is turned on, the infant hears a recording of intrauterine sounds similar to what he experienced before birth. A ticking clock can also provide a rhythmic background against which other stimulation can occur.

Within the first few weeks after birth, we can put small

music boxes covered with satin or other soft fabric in the crib. Eden's Wagging Musicals, small windup musical animals made of softest plush with heads that gently move back and forth, are also good. Initially these toys just provide the infant with a pleasant sound. Later they will play a role in the important process of the child's learning to follow a sound. You can hold the music box or Wagging Musical a few inches from the infant's face for a short period of time. Then you move the musical toy to either side of the infant's face to get him to turn his head in the direction of the sound. You might have to help by gently turning the infant's head for him at first.

Musical mobiles such as the Fisher-Price Music Mobile can be hung over the crib. At first the toy will just provide auditory stimulation, but later when the child is pulling up and reaching toward the sound, he may discover the objects hanging from the mobile. This mobile has animals and a farmer that are attached by a nylon cord strong enough to prevent the child from pulling them off. The cord is also short enough so that there is little or no danger of the child's getting tangled up in it.

After the infant can grasp under his own conscious volition (about 4 or 5 months), he can repeatedly be given the music box or Wagging Musicals in his hands in order to encourage grasping. Because the visually handicapped infant does not have the visual stimulus of the desired object to excite him into reaching and grasping for it, you must initiate the process. Encourage your child to reach for the musical toy by allowing him to hold it for a short time and then taking it away. Then hold the toy a short distance away from your child, and as he is learning to locate an object by its sound, he may be encouraged to reach for the toy. When the music box and Wagging Musicals are put in his hands, the child is getting information through his sense of touch as well as through his ears. The music box should be silky or soft. The plush Wagging Musicals are soft, and the child will be able to feel the gently swaying movements of their heads.

Infants will also get varied tactile and auditory stimulation from a rattle, depending on its shape and sound. For the visually handicapped infant it may be a good idea to have a number of rattles that make a variety of sounds and have a variety of shapes. For example, plastic keys on a chain will have a different clatter than a small plastic rattle, which will sound different from a large plastic rattle, which will sound different from a set of wooden rings on a dowel. The greater the child's auditory discrimination ability, the better he or she will be able to cope with and adapt to the environment. Rattles can also be used to get the infant to follow a sound from side to side even before he is able to grasp a rattle.

As the infant achieves the feats of following an object by its sound and reaching for and grasping it, the parents must convey their pleasure and excitement by the sound, tone, and inflection of their voices, along with hugging, touching, and cuddling. The child will not, of course, be able to tell his parents' reactions by seeing their pleased expressions.

As the child is able to sit up on his own in the crib, one of the following might be attached:

- Kohner's Busy Box
- Gabriel's Busy Box
- Gabriel's Disney Musical Busy Box
- Fisher's-Price's Activity Center

You will have to start the child's interaction with this type of toy by taking his hands and helping him to touch it. For the blind infant, exploration with the hands is always a necessary prelude to an experience with a new toy. After the child has explored the busy box and is aware of its presence, he can then be taught to operate each of the individual toys on its surface.

In order to internalize the basic concept of cause and effect ("I can produce a change in my environment, I can produce something, my behavior matters"), the infant must be given many experiences with toys that allow him to make a connection between his behavior (the cause) and what the toy does (the effect). The following toys give the child a chance to do something and produce some auditory effect, something that the child can hear:

- Rattles and teethers that make a sound when moved
- Crib gyms, which have loops through which the infant can stick his foot or hand and produce a ringing sound by shaking the loops.
- The previously mentioned busy boxes, which have items that ring, buzz, click, or produce some other sound when manipulated.
- Playskool's Baby Flutter Balls and Fisher-Price's Chime Ball; not only do these balls give the infant experience with cause and effect, but they also allow him to follow and locate and object by its sound.
- Squeeze toys that make a sound when chewed on or pressed. (Make a safety check before buying these—the squeaker should be completely enclosed in the toy and be unlikely to be exposed or come apart.)
- Fisher-Price's Turn and Learn Activity Center

If the infant is partially sighted, the all-important self-awareness toy, a safety mirror, should be used just as it is for the fully sighted child. Mirrors are found on Fisher-Price's Flower Rattle, Fisher-Price's Turn and Learn Activity Center, and some of the busy boxes.

When the infant is sitting alone very competently and enjoys his bath, you can introduce tub and pool toys such as Fisher-Price's Bath Activity Center, Three Men In A Tub, Floating Family, Snap Lock Beads, and any other plastic toys that will float. Try to choose toys that have distinctive shapes and complex, varying textures.

During infancy, the child gains a perception of himself as a physical entity bounded by skin, having hands that he can make move, and so forth. The visually handicapped infant should be encouraged to touch and explore the parts of his body, as well as his parents' faces and later the faces of other members of the family. It is important for the parent to say the correct word for each part of the body as it is touched, even though the infant does not yet have the verbal skills to repeat the word. In late infancy, before he can verbalize the words (words that he understands and can actually say are called his active vocabulary), he is capable of understanding them. Words that he can understand fairly easily but cannot say are called his passive vocabulary. From late infancy onward, the child's passive vocabulary is always greater than his active vocabulary; that is, the child can always understand many more words than he can actually say at any particular time. Thus adults should not severely limit their vocabulary when talking with children even though they cannot repeat or give an explanation of many of the words used. This is one way that the vocabulary of the sighted as well as the blind child expands and grows. As the blind child learns the parts of the body, the game of "show me the eyes, ears, feet" can be played with a three-dimensional doll rather than a picture. (Don't ask the child to point out a doll's features until after he has had ample time to explore the doll with his hands.)

The game can also be played with stuffed animals of all kinds—bears, dogs, cats, ducks, monkeys, etc.—so that the child is not only getting an idea of the different configurations of the features of various animals, but is also learning that all animals have some things in common and some things that are different.

Plush stuffed animals are excellent to give the toddler during the second year, after he has stopped putting things into his mouth constantly. The first year, when the mouth is such an important channel of sensory information about the environment, chewable stuffed toys—toys that won't shed, aren't long haired or furry, and are completely washable, such as Fisher-Price's Cholly and Lolly, Peek-A-Boo Baby, Security Bunny, and Animal Grabbers—are best.

The need to build, to construct, to create can be fostered initially by the use of interlocking blocks. These blocks fit into and/or connect to each other and cannot be accidentally disassembled as easily as other blocks. The larger, easier-to-handle blocks are for the younger child. As he gets older, develops greater manual dexterity, and has more control in the small muscles of his fingers, he can then manipulate the smaller blocks. Good choices in interlocking blocks include:

- Entex's Loc Blocs
- Lego Systems' Duplo and later the smaller Lego blocks
- Mattel's Tuff Stuff Wonder Blocks
- Playskool's Bristle Blocks and Bristle Bears

In early childhood, the youngster will enjoy the more complex interlocking toys such as Gabriel's Tinkertoys, Lincoln Logs, and Highland's Ramaggon.

Other toys that foster manual dexterity and help stimulate mental development include:

- Playskool's Wooden Beads for stringing (can also be used with plastic containers for classification exercises; that is, putting all of the oblong beads in one container, all of the round beads in another)
- Playskool's Stacking Discs
- Fisher-Price's Rock-A-Stack, Baby's First Blocks, Shape Sorter
- Playskool's Shape Sorting Box, Teddy-Bear Shape Sorter Work Bench
- Fisher-Price's Wood Top Work Bench
- Playskool's Nesting Assortment of Eggs, Barrels, Drums, and Cubes
- Playskool's Counting Frame

The puzzles that are most easily used by the blind child are not regular jigsaw puzzles, but those that consist of a few individual pieces that fit into discrete, separate places on the puzzle board. Playskool has a series of "First Puzzles" that include nine different wooden puzzles, such as a banana, an apple, and a bunch of grapes, each with four pieces. The outlines of the individual fruits will give the information needed to find the correct spaces on the puzzle board. Other excellent puzzles are Playskool's Form Board and Fisher-Price's Farm Animals, Vehicles, Nursery Rhymes, and Animal Friends. The Fisher-Price puzzles are also good choices because they have small plastic knobs attached to the puzzle pieces that allow for easy removal and replacement.

The Creative Parenting Institute (P.O. Box 55258, Fort Washington, Maryland 20744) is currently involved in a project to produce tactile jigsaw puzzles and braille blocks, as well as other children's playthings. Contact the Institute for further information about these.

Wooden pegboards with short, cylindrical pegs give the child excellent opportunities for manipulation and, maybe even more important, provide an introduction to the various configurations of braille bumps—a valuable reading readiness skill. Playskool and Ideal make good pegboards of this kind.

To help the child learn to dress himself, the Dressy Bessy and Dapper Dan dolls by Playskool are very useful. Parents must praise the child when he masters the manipulations necessary to dress the doll, and when he achieves success with his own clothes. It's also important to *tell* the child just what it is that he has done, such as, "Fantastic, now you have snapped up your jacket!"

*Physical Development*

The blind infant may begin walking a little later than his sighted counterpart, but usually the feat is accomplished at some time during the second year. When the child is securely mobile, he can be introduced to ride-on and push toys. Because these toys extend some distance in front of the child, they will afford him a measure of safety. Push toys that facilitate the development of the large muscles of the arms and legs used in locomotion include Fisher-Price's Push-Along Clown (which also demonstrates cause and effect), Push

Chime, Corn Popper, and Melody Push Chime, and Playskool's Letter Block Wagon.

Ride-on toys that are propelled by the toddler's own foot power include:

- Fisher-Price's Little Red Riding Wagon, Riding Horse, Creative Coaster, Explorer
- Playskool's Big Yellow Toddler Taxi, Toddler Truck, Tyke Bike
- Empire's Tot-A-Bout Trike, Tot-A-Bout Car
- Wonder's Bucky The Horse, Scooter Frog, Walk-R-Ride
- Little Tike's Tike Wagon, Ollie Coaster

As the toddler gains greater physical prowess, we can introduce him to the Little Wheels vehicles and also to hobbyhorses or rocking horses.

When the child first tries out large toys such as the ride-on toys, it is very important that he perceive the entire object so that he has more than just a fragmented concept of it. Therefore, the parent should take the child's hands and move them all over the toy before putting him onto it.

## Musical Toys

Two kinds of musical toys that the child manipulates can be introduced during the second year. With the first type, the child turns the toy on and operates it so that he is entertained with music: these include Fisher-Price's Change-A-Tune Carousel and Tote-A-Tune Music Box Radio. With the second type, the child manipulates the toy to produce the music himself. Toy pianos, toy xylophones, tambourines, and maracas are good to start. Later, such instruments as the triangle and those found in the Fisher-Price Rhythm Band are good choices, as are harmonicas, toy pianos, thumbnail pianos (Kalimbas), records, guitars, and—if the parents can stand them—drums.

As the blind toddler moves into early childhood (ages 2–6), the record player and cassette tape recorder will be very important audio toys. Fisher-Price makes a sturdy tape recorder designed to take the less-than-delicate handling of young owners. General Electric, Vanity Fair, and Fisher-Price all make good children's record players that are simple to operate. Some children 4 years old, and certainly those 5 years of age, can handle records, record players, cassette tapes, and tape recorders well enough to operate them independently.

Record and cassette players can be used with talking books as well as for music. The visually handicapped child will greatly appreciate recordings of nursery rhymes, sing-along records, and stories with sound effects. They will be rich auditory experiences. Today, with the ready availability of recorders and cassettes, parents can tape for playback familiar sounds that occur within the child's environment, as well as favorite stories.

## An Introduction to Books

Bedtime story reading is as important for the blind child as it is for all others, and this process should begin in infancy. Tactile cloth alphabet books containing objects that the child can touch (E is for elastic, F is for fur, etc.) are available from the Volunteers for the Visually Handicapped at 4405 East-West Highway, Bethesda, Maryland. The Golden Fragrance Books are an excellent example of books that appeal to senses other than the visual. Throughout each of these books are places where the child can scratch and smell the particular fragrance that is associated with the activity at that point in the story. Titles in the Golden Fragrance Books series include:

*Bambi's Fragrant Forest*
*Detective Arthur on the Scent*
*Little Bunny Follows His Nose*
*Max the Nosey Bear*

*A Nose for Trouble*
*See No Evil, Hear No Evil, Smell No Evil*
*The Sweet Smell of Christmas*
*The Winnie the Pooh Scratch and Sniff Book*

The National Library Service for the Blind and Physically Handicapped at the Library of Congress has catalogs of thousands of books that are available in braille and on records and cassette tapes. These braille and talking books as well as tape recorders and record players are available free of charge by mail to anyone who has a temporary or permanent visual disability that precludes his utilizing the printed word. One catalog (available in braille and regular print) is a compendium of all of the books for younger readers along with the suggested ages or grade levels. Order forms come with the catalogs. If you need additional information concerning the eligibility requirements, procedures, and participating libraries, check with your local library or write to the National Library Service for the Blind and Physically Handicapped, Library of Congress, Washington, D.C. 20542.

*Recognition and Reading Skills*

Teaching the child to recognize various small objects is an excellent game to play during the day or as an alternative to storytime at night. Small wooden, plastic, and vinyl objects can be placed in a "grab bag" adapted perhaps from a laundry bag, a basket, or a medium-sized plastic wastebasket. The objects can be changed as the child becomes familiar with them and can name them.

Blind children seem to be able to understand early on that some of the objects they handle are miniature replicas of life-sized objects. You might include in the grab bag some of the small wooden or plastic cars, trucks, animals, people, dishes and cups, or fruits and vegetables that are available. When playing with the grab bag animals, you can introduce the child to the different sounds they make once he can identify them by name. The rigid plastic horses made by Breyer Molding Company are particularly good buys. Not only will the child get a feel for the configuration of the horse, but the figures are proportionally accurate. (When choosing toys for the grab bag, it is best to get ones that are more or less proportionally accurate rather than ones that are distorted, that have particularly long limbs, for example.)

By the time the child is into early childhood, a small, sturdy wooden table and chair, such as those made by Childcraft, are very important tools. They will provide a work/play surface and seat low enough so that the risk of the child's falling off and hurting himself is minimal. With the table, chair, and the toy grab bag, we now have an instant "reading readiness skills center." The same grab bag objects that were used for basic recognition can also be used in the development of skills that the child will need for reading.

First, you and the child can play the game of matching two identical objects. Put the mates of one half of the objects into the grab bag. Then give the child one of the remaining objects, allow him to explore it, then have him reach into the grab bag and secure its mate.

Another simple matching game can be created by cutting out two matching swatches of tactile materials and pasting them onto small squares of poster board. Cotton, satin, corduroy, sandpaper, and velvet dotted swiss are good choices. The child is then given one of the squares and asked to feel and find its mate in the cards on the table in front of him. As the child becomes familiar with this game, the matching could become less varied and more difficult, thereby helping the child develop a highly sensitive sense of touch.

The grab bag objects can be used in the development of another reading readiness skill, that of classification. The child can be asked, after the initial exploration, to put together in a group all of the animals that live on a farm, all those that live in a zoo, all of the fruits, all the things that we eat, the things that we ride in, and so on.

## Artistic Development

The need to create artistically can be satisfied in various ways. The child can experiment with finger-painting. Finger paint is made commercially by Crayola. It can also be made at home using old-fashioned cooked starch and powdered tempera paint, which is available from any artist's supply store or educational supply store if it cannot be located in the toy store. Sand and other granulated materials can be added to the paint to provide an even richer tactile surface when the paint dries.

The Creative Parenting Institute (see page 144) offers a special coloring kit called Kolor Kastles. It is a plastic sheet molded with outlines of letters and appropriate objects ("A" for apple, for example), along with braille dots. The child colors within the outline using crayons or paint, and can then feel what he has colored. The plastic can be wiped off and reused.

Pipe cleaners are an easily accessible, inexpensive material for free-form sculptures. Clay, plasticine, and Adica Pongó's Pongo are also materials that allow the child to explore creatively, using only the sense of touch. Don't use molds. Let the child structure his own creature by molding with his fingers, or with tongue depressors, or with other blunt sculpting tools.

Collages can be made from tactually interesting pieces, giving the child an excellent opportunity to get experience cutting and pasting, arranging the pieces, and enjoying and differentiating among the textures.

Directions for making "Touch Pictures" as well as other touch toys and games are given in a seventy-seven-page booklet developed by volunteers working with the visually handicapped. This booklet is available for $3 plus 60 cents to cover postage and handling, from Touch Toys (D and D Duplicating), P.O. Box 2224, Rockville, Maryland 20852.

## Stimulating Electronic Toys

While most computer toys demand a certain level of eye-hand coordination, some feature games that depend at least partially on auditory cues. These games can be played by the visually handicapped child. For instance, Parker Brothers' Merlin, an electronic toy that has been programmed to play six games, has ten small, numbered windows that make a particular sound and flash a red light when touched. In one of the games, Echo, the player chooses a number from two to ten. If the number is three, the computer will flash a random pattern of three red lights in different windows accompanied by three different sounds. The player then repeats the pattern of lights and sounds. If he is correct, the computer will respond with an auditory "victory call." If he is incorrect, a different set of auditory stimuli is heard. Initially the blind child can experiment with the computer until he learns the placement of the sounds that are associated with each window. He can begin playing the game of Echo with a series of two or three sounds, and increase the number of sounds as he masters each level. The visually handicapped child can also play Merlin's Music Man. In this game, the player punches in a series of sounds and the computer plays it back for him. Milton Bradley's Simon and Encore's Mimic Me are other examples of computer games in which the auditory cues given are sufficient for the playing of the game.

Speak and Spell by Texas Instruments is an excellent electronic toy that can be used by the blind child. After he has learned the placement of the letters on the keyboard, he can begin to spell words by pressing the appropriate letter keys. For instance, a voice will say "spell WONDER." As the child presses each letter key, it is repeated auditorily. If he makes a mistake, there is an erase button. After he completes the word, he is given immediate auditory feedback as to whether or not the spelling of the word was correct.

Mattel's Magical Thing produces a wide range of musical tones when the child presses designated points on the toy.

Information concerning other games that are designed for or can be adapted for the visually handicapped is available from the American Council for the Blind, 1211 Connecticut Avenue, N.W., Suite 506, Washington, D.C. 20036.

Toys and play practices that are used in social and dramatic play are essentially the same for the visually handicapped as for the sighted child. The material contained in chapters 5 and 6 and the section on dramatic play in chapter 4 applies for the blind child with only minor—if any—modifications.

## Children with Other Disabilities

There are a number of organizations and publications that should prove useful to parents of disabled children in helping them make necessary adjustments. The parents of hearing-impaired children can contact:

Alexander Graham Bell Association for the Deaf
3417 Volta Place, N.W.
Washington, D.C. 20007

National Association of the Deaf
814 Thayer Ave.
Silver Spring, Md. 20910

Paul W. Ogden and Suzanne Lipsett's *The Silent Garden: Understanding the Hearing Impaired Child* (New York: St. Martin's Press, 1982) is a fine treatment of the subject and, among other areas it covers, contains many ideas for fostering your child's development through books, toys, and play.

Parents of children with other disabilities may find the following good sources of information:

Association for the Aid of Crippled Children
345 E. 46th St.
New York, N.Y. 10017

Closer Look
1201 16th St., N.W.
Suite 607E
Washington, D.C. 20036

Office of Education
Bureau of Education for the Handicapped
Washington, D.C. 20201

The National Easter Seal Society
 for Crippled Children and Adults
2023 W. Ogden Ave.
Chicago, Ill. 60612

National Foundation for Birth Defects
800 Second St.
New York, N.Y. 10017

Ayrault, Evelyn West. *Growing Up Handicapped.* New York: Seabury Press, 1977.
Hart, Verna. *Beginning with the Handicapped.* Springfield, Ill.: Charles C. Thomas, 1974.
Spock, Benjamin, and Marion O. Lerrigo. *Caring for Your Disabled Child.* New York: Macmillan, 1965.

## *The Sick Child*

It is well known that adults derive great benefits from recreational and occupational therapy. The same is true of play and toys for the sick child. Play can diminish restrictive feelings and restlessness. It can also improve the child's mental state, which can be a significant factor in facilitating the healing process. The physical activity of play can improve circulation and help prevent the muscle weakness that occurs as a result of nonusage.

There may be significant changes in a child's behavior when he is ill. For one thing, his attention span may be shorter, and there may be a need to rotate the toys and play activities more frequently than usual. In fact, the parent may have to take the initiative in changing the play activities, whereas the child would do so himself if he were well.

The child's energy level may be lower and he may tire more easily. He will probably not have the physical or mental stamina to meet new play challenges. So this is not the best time to introduce a difficult new puzzle, book, or game. The toys he uses should make limited physical demands on him.

When your child is ill, he may not act as mature as he usually does. He may want more parental attention and reassurance. You may find it difficult to meet these increased demands but should remember that they are temporary. It is sometimes helpful to put a clock in the child's room set to go off on the hour. When the alarm goes off, you can spend fifteen or twenty minutes of undivided time with the child, changing the toys, reading to him, and so on.

It is a good idea to have a few toys in a "bed box" that are brought out only when the child is ill. These should be toys that are just a little beneath his normal developmental level so that he will not be frustrated by them. The bed box can include solitary play, inexpensive toys that are kept ready for a time of illness, such as:

- a small table village and blocks
- paper dolls
- a new set of crayons, colored pencils, or magic markers, and paper
- books of Altair Designs (published by Pantheon, these are excellent for the 5- or 6-year-old to the adolescent. Their originator came up with the idea while in bed recuperating from a car accident.)
- old magazines for cutting up to make collages
- needlepoint, sewing, or other craft kits appropriate to the age of the child
- a small 3½-by-3½-inch puzzle for the older child, or one with a difficulty level lower than the child is used to
- origami kit
- paperback books
- easy model kit of a car, boat, airplane, etc.

After playing with the toys during his illness, the child might insist on continuing to play with them. This is why we want to keep the bed box stocked with inexpensive items that can be replaced without wrecking the yearly toy budget. A bed table or bed tray that provides a rigid, flat surface is also a must. And the old hospital practice of folding down a paper bag and pinning it to the bed is especially good for trash and waste paper that accumulates.

In addition to the bed box contents, the following toys are good ones for the sick child, even though they will also be available during other times.

## Creative Toys

>   scissors
>   paste
>   colored construction paper
>   popsicle sticks
>   bits of wood for creative structures and collages
>   weaving loom
>   magnetic alphabets and numbers
>   beads and string

>   For the older child:

>   mosaic art kits
>   leathercraft kits
>   string art
>   macrame

## Construction Toys

>   Duplo and Lego (Lego Systems)
>   Loc Blocs (Entex)
>   Bristle Bears and Blocks (Playskool)
>   play tiles
>   parquetry blocks
>   pegboards and pegs
>   shape-sorting toys

stacking cups or cubes
puzzles such as Rubik's Cube

For the older child:

Capsela (Playjour)
Ramaggon (Highland)

## *Dramatic Play Toys*

dolls and accessories
small cars and other vehicles
finger and arm puppets
play people sets such as farm, hospital, airport, garage, etc.

## *Musical Toys*

records and record players
tapes and tape recorders. (Make up a tape for the child, giving him directions to complete certain play activities in the forty-minute solitary time. These play projects can then be examined in the twenty-minute "together time.")
musical instruments
movie cartridges and viewer
View master and cards (by GAF)

## *Examination and Exploration Toys*

magnets
kaleidoscope
magnifying glass
binoculars
books

## Electronic Games

Simon (Milton Bradley)
Mimic Me (Encore)
Merlin (Parker Brothers)
Speak and Spell (Texas Instruments)
sports games such as baseball, hockey, etc.

## Card and Board Games (for visitor time and together time with the parent)

Candyland (Milton Bradley)
Chutes and Ladders (Milton Bradley)
Uno (International Games)
Chinese checkers
chess
Old Maid (Milton Bradley and other manufacturers)
Monopoly (Parker Brothers)

While the child is ill, we do want to keep him occupied and involved with play activities rather than encouraging a lot of television viewing, which is harmful for two reasons. First, the child is sitting there passively watching the set and may not be moving around as much as he would without the television. Increasingly, doctors are seeing the benefits of mild physical exertion during illness and convalescence. Of course, parents will have to monitor this closely and be aware of the irritability that develops in the young child as he becomes tired without realizing it. The second reason is that very few of the daytime TV programs are geared to or suitable for the young audience.

While we realize the need for making the surroundings and the playtime experiences as pleasant as possible in order to speed recovery, we do not want to make the period of illness overly enjoyable. If the child gets too many wonderful new toys and too much special attention, he may see a kind of reward in being sick, and may try to do it more frequently.

## *The Hospitalized Child*

Many hospitals recognize the therapeutic value of play and toys, and there may be on the pediatric ward a well-stocked playroom and recreation area. There may also be on the staff a Child Life Director, whose role is to coordinate the play activities of the children on the ward.

The anxieties of hospitalized children who are awaiting various surgical procedures and/or treatments seem to be somewhat relieved by allowing them to play with medical toys. They help the child verbalize and deal with fears associated with the illness and the impending surgical procedures, as well as painful feelings that may be the aftermath of treatment. These might include:

> miniature hospital set, which will contain various medical machines, an operating room, miniature doctors and nurses, miniature ambulances, etc.
> toy doctor's kits
> toy stethoscope
> toy hypodermic needles and dolls to which shots are given
> child-sized nurse's caps
> disposable surgical masks
> surgical gloves
> gauze and bandages
> Band-Aids
> pill boxes
> tongue depressors
> arm and finger puppets

Many hospitals in conjunction with the local Board of Education will have hospital-based teachers who will give the child individual instruction while he is in the hospital. If the hospital provides adequately for the academic and play needs of the child, it might not be necessary to take in a great many of the child's own toys. You might check with hospital personnel regarding the kinds and number of toys that should be brought from home.

If you are sending a toy to a hospitalized child, it is probably best to give something small such as a book or game that can be used either alone or in activities with another child while in the hospital, and which can then make the transition to a home toy.

Silly novelty toys that evoke laughter and that you would not normally buy, such as a set of chattering false teeth, might be good choices for the older hospitalized child.

When my then 10-year-old was hospitalized for nine weeks for a possibly life-threatening case of systemic juvenile rheumatoid arthritis, one of the most pleasurable gifts that he received was a large box that had about eight or nine small wrapped packages in it with explicit directions on each to open one a day. One said, "Open this package when the nurse won't come after you have rung for her," and in the package was a goose horn. "Open this when your mom has nothing to do on those long hospital evenings"—and there was a book on people who were millionaires by age 35. "Open this package for your dad after he has spent a sleepless night at the hospital"—and in it was a can of warm beer. "Open this when you feel like writing," and in it was a notebook and pen with a note encouraging him to keep a journal of his hospital stay, writing down the feelings he had about the things that happened to him. In another, which said, "Open me when you feel like reading," there was a book of the story of Robin Hood. When he opened that present, he really did not feel like reading himself, but he enjoyed my reading it to him, and sometimes it would soothe him to the point of sleep. I was overjoyed one day when I asked if he wanted me to read him another chapter and he replied with a small smile playing around his lips, "I hate to tell you this, Mom, but I finished reading it by myself." After my expression of exaggerated disappointment, he said, "It was so exciting, I couldn't wait." Fortunately, he recovered completely with the wonderful medical treatment that he received, but play, books, and toys contributed a most supportive part.

# 10
# Homemade Playthings

Years ago most toys were made at home, but today, because of mass production, very few children play with homemade toys. Growing concern about the quality of toys, as well as the spiraling cost, may soon contribute to a small reversal of this phenomenon. There will not, however, be a widespread return to homemade toys because of the expense of making one individual item, the cost of the materials that must be purchased, and the significant amount of time needed. As more and more mothers are working outside the home, there will be less time available for activities such as toy making. Those toys that *are* homemade will be a "labor of love" that is done in spite of time, cost, and efficiency.

If you would like to create original, homemade toys, here are a few simple projects to get you started. At the end of the chapter is a list of project books for further reading and inspiration.

### Baby's First Cloth Picture Book

#### Items Needed

- ½ to 1 yard of white cotton sailcloth
- 8½-by-11-inch drawing paper

- fabric crayons (Milton Bradley)
- pinking shears
- large needle and thread
- iron

## Method

Cut the material into 8-by-8-inch pieces with the pinking shears. Draw simple letters and whatever objects you like on the paper with the fabric crayons. Iron the pictures onto the fabric pages and put the pages together. Stitch up the left side with the thread, using a simple running stitch.

## *Bean Bag*

### *Items Needed*

- fabric
- beans—black-eyed peas or any small beans
- sewing machine or needle and thread

## *Method*

Take any gingham or solid fabric and double the material. Draw a simple gingerbread boy or a circle for a person's face with a magic marker. Embroider the features onto the cloth. Cut out the figure, leaving about 3/8-inch for a hem. Stitch up the bag either on the machine or by hand with an overcasting stitch, leaving one side open. Fill the bag with beans. Close the opening with an overcast stitch.

To make stuffed animals, dolls, or puppets, you can get patterns from companies such as McCall's, Vogue, Simplicity, and Butterick. Most fabric departments carry felt and furry fabric, so that the puppets and stuffed animals can have the proper texture.

## *Number Puzzles and Alphabet Tiles*

### *Items Needed*

- a 4-by-4-inch piece of cabinet-grade wood, cut into 3-inch strips at the lumberyard (The thickness of the wood doesn't matter, as long as it is at least ⅛-inch thick. The thinner the wood, the less expensive it is.)
- electric hand-held jigsaw or manual coping saw
- C-clamps
- electric sander or sandpaper (If you are planning to go on making wooden toys, an electric sander is a must.)
- number and letter stencils or iron-on embroidery letters and numbers (The letter stencils can be purchased in any educational supply store, and the iron-on embroidery letters and numbers at a needlecraft store.)
- patterns for geometric shapes (circles, triangles, squares, rectangles, pentagons, etc.)
- brightly colored nontoxic paints and paintbrushes, or permanent magic markers

### *Number Puzzles*

Take two of the 3-inch strips and cut them into ten pieces to make ten number puzzles. Sand the front, back, and edges of each piece so there will be rounded edges and no splinters.

Stencil in or iron on the numbers 1, 2, 3, etc., at the top of each piece, one number on each piece of wood. Next, trace in pencil the appropriate number of geometric designs at the bottom of each puzzle piece. Draw a free-form, wavy pencil line across the middle of the puzzle between the number and the shapes. Brace the pieces of wood on both sides with scrap wood and attach them to a stationary surface with C-clamps.

With the coping saw or jigsaw, cut across the wavy lines. Sand the edges of the interconnecting pieces. Paint in or color the numerals and geometric shapes.

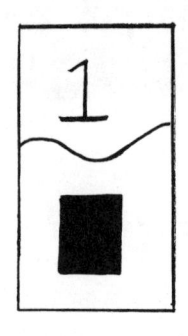

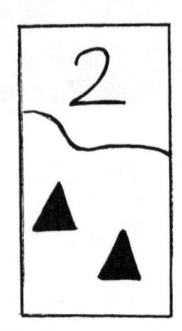

You might want to paint the number and its corresponding puzzle piece the same color. If you do, the puzzle will be easier for young children, as color seems to be their most important cue with regard to reorganizing and classifying. However, the child may then be learning primarily which colors on the puzzle pieces match, rather than which number corresponds with which group of shapes. Thus, you might make all the numbers one color and vary the colors of the geometric shapes.

### *Mobile Alphabet Tiles*

Use the remainder of the 3-inch strips to cut 3-by-3-inch squares. Sand the edges. Set aside about half of the squares to be painted with lowercase letters later. Stencil in or iron on capital letters on the rest of the tiles. Make several of each vowel and the more frequently used consonants. Paint the letters in a variety of colors; however, be sure to make all the same letters the same color.

There are a number of reading readiness games that can be played with these tiles. Put out several of them and ask your child to match or put together all the letters that are the same color. You will have several different kinds of letters in this group if you have used only seven or eight different colors of paint. Then ask your child to look at the red letters and put all of the As together; all of the Is together; and so on. Next put three tiles together, such as A, B, and another A, and ask your child to choose the one that is different. This will help teach him about differentiation and matching.

The tiles can be used to teach the sounds that each letter makes, and to encourage your child to think of some words that begin with those particular sounds. After the sounds have been mastered, he can begin making short words with the tiles.

Since the configuration and shapes of the lowercase letters are so different from their capital counterparts, learning them is really like learning a second alphabet. Use the remaining half of the pieces of wood to make lowercase alphabet tiles. Paint the letters the same colors you painted the capitals, so that when you play the game of matching capital to small letter, different colors will not be a distraction.

Finally, when the lowercase alphabet has been learned as well as the capital letters, the child can begin making short sentences. He may not have the manual dexterity to write with a pencil yet, but sentences are easy to make with the alphabet tiles. These tiles will last for a number of years and can be made to serve a variety of purposes.

## *For Further Reading*

The following books may also prove helpful for creating homemade toys.

> Caney, Steven. *Steven Caney's Toy Book.* New York: Workman Publishing Co., 1972.
> Cogne, John, and Miller, Jerry. *How to Make Upside Down Dolls.* New York: Bobbs-Merrill Co., 1978.
> Editors of Sunset Books and Sunset Magazine. *Soft Toys and Dolls.* Menlo Park, Calif.: Lane Publishing Co., 1977.
> Farnsworth, Warren. *Folk Toys and How to Make Them.* Toronto: Clark, Irwin and Co., 1974.
> Fremlin-Key, Hermyone. *More Toys and Gifts for You to Make.* Newton Centre, Mass.: Charles T. Branford Co., 1971.
> Gogniat, Maurice. *Wild West Toys You Can Make.* New York: Sterling Publishing Co., 1976.

Greenhowe, Jean. *Jean Greenhowe's Miniature Toys.* New York: Van Nostrand, Reinhold Co., 1980.

Heady, Eleanor B. *Make Your Own Dolls.* New York: Lothrop, Lee and Shep Co., 1974.

Holz, Loretta. *The How-To Book of International Dolls: A Comprehensive Guide to Making, Costuming and Collecting Dolls.* New York: Crown Publishers, 1980.

Hutchings, Margaret. *Teddy Bears and How to Make Them.* New York: Dover Publications, 1977.

———. *Toys from the Tales of Beatrix Potter.* New York: F. Warne and Co., 1973.

Janitch, Valerie. *Dolls in Miniature.* Radnor, Pa.: Chilton Book Co., 1976.

Joseph, Joan. *Folk Toys around the World and How to Make Them.* New York: Parents Magazine Press in cooperation with U. S. Committee for UNICEF, 1972.

Laury, Jean Ray, and Law, Ruth M. *Homemade Toys and Games, A Guide to Creating Your Own.* New York: Doubleday and Co., 1975.

Maginley, C. J. *Trains and Boats and Planes and . . . Custom Building Wooden Toys.* New York: Hawthorn Books, 1979.

Morton, Brenda. *Do-It-Yourself Dinosaurs: Imaginative Toy Craft for Beginners.* New York: Taplinger Publishing Co., 1973.

Peppe, Rodney. *Rodney Peppe's Moving Toys.* New York: Sterling Publishing Co., 1980.

Peterson, Frank Lynn. *Children's Toys You Can Build Yourself.* Englewood Cliffs, N.J.: Prentice-Hall, 1978.

Provenso, Eugene and Asterie. *The Historian's Toy Box: Children's Toys from the Past You Can Make Yourself.* New York: Prentice-Hall, 1979.

Rath, Erna. *The Splendid Soft Toy Book.* New York: Sterling Publishing Co., 1981.

Rose, Ethne. *Dolls.* New York: Charles Scribner's Sons, 1979.

Roth, Charlene Davis. *The Art of Making Puppets and*

*Marionettes*. Radnor, Pa.: Chilton Book Co., 1975.

Russell, Joan. *The Woman's Day Book of Soft Toys and Dolls*. New York: Simon and Schuster, 1975.

Staples, Caroline. *The Yarn Animal Book*. New York: Simon and Schuster, 1976.

Supraner, Robyn and Lauren. *Plenty of Puppets to Make*. Mahwah, N.J.: Troll Associates, 1981.

Swan, Sara K. *Homemade Baby Toys*. Boston: Houghton, Mifflin, Co., 1977.

Verkist, Susan. *Crocheted Toys and Dolls: Complete Instructions for Twelve Easy to Do Projects*. New York: Dover Publications, 1978.

Williams, J. Alan. *The Kids and Grown Ups' Toy Making Book*. New York: William Morrow and Co., 1979.

# 11
# Toys and Television Advertising

Much of the impetus for children asking their parents to buy specific toys, particularly around Christmas, comes from the impact of television toy commercials. A 1979 Nielsen study stated that the average child under 12 spends approximately twenty-seven hours per week watching television. By the time the typical child in our society graduates from high school, he has spent some 22,000 hours in front of a television set—more time than he has spent in school. He has also seen an estimated 350,000 commercials, a significant portion of them for toys.

Though today almost all children's programming on commercial television is sponsored, this has not always been the case. When television first appeared on the scene, the major thrust was in the area of market development, the creation of a large audience of viewers. The most effective way to get prospective viewers to buy a set was to provide excellent program material. This included superb programming for children, of which about half was presented without sponsors. According to William Melody in *Children's Television: The Economics of Exploitation*, in 1950 the four networks, ABC, CBS, NBC, and the now nonexistent DuMont network, provided on the average about twenty-seven hours of children's programming per week. Typically there were children's programs in the weekday evening time slot from 6 to 8 P.M.

This method of building audience size through excellent programming worked very well—it is estimated that between the years of 1949 and 1952 the number of television sets in the homes of viewers increased from about 190,000 to more than 16 million. The 1980 Census shows that there are now approximately 86 million television sets in the United States.

The increasing ownership of TV sets was a factor in the shift from providing programming that appealed primarily to viewers to providing programming that would appeal to sponsors. Initially, some sponsors would own a particular show and exercise some control over the content of the program. Sponsors bought specific shows to appeal to certain audiences. Children were not considered a target audience because they did not make the purchases, and so programming aimed at adults began to dominate weekday evening schedules.

In America the commercial programming is determined by the "largest share of the audience" concept and the "counterprogramming" idea. The largest share of the audience concept refers to the fact that programming in a certain time slot is geared to the largest segment of the total audience watching at that time. Even though there may be large numbers of children watching in the evening hours, there are even more adults, and so the programming and advertising are directed toward adults. This explains why, even though there are fewer children watching television on weekday mornings than weekday evenings, it is the mornings that offer more children's programming.

In a 1975 study done by Dr. F. Earle Barcus for Action for Children's Television, it was found that there was a greater number of commercials in programs designed for children's viewing than would be found in the same length of prime-time television. Of the commercials monitored during weekend children's programming, advertising for toys made up 18 percent of the total. The toy category was second only to the "cereals, candies, and other sweets" category, which accounted for 25 percent of the total. During the holiday season, however, toys tended to dominate the commercials.

Though they do not usually buy the products themselves, children can strongly influence those who do, and therefore they have become a very profitable "target audience." Some people feel that it is unethical to direct advertising to children because of their inability to understand in adult terms. Others accept commercials as part of the viewing package and may even see them as an educational tool by which the child can learn some of the rules of the marketplace.

### *How Commercials Work*

Dr. Barcus found in his 1975 study of toy commercials that:

1. The most frequently advertised toys are dolls and cars. Typically, girls are playing with dolls and boys are playing with cars.
2. Ninety percent of the commercials for toys use live action; that is, children playing with the toys rather than animation. (This is easy to understand if we know that younger children tend to learn the general "rule" that live action is *real* and cartoons or animation is *pretend*.)
3. Over 90 percent of the toy advertisements used the "voice-over" technique; that is, having an off-stage announcer who is not actually seen in the film, narrating the action of the commercial.
4. Over half of the commercials were for two or more items that were sold separately.

Also, according to Dr. Barcus's study, there are some technical filming factors that can contribute to an unrealistic perception of the toy by a young child since his understanding of these effects would be limited. Camera close-ups might cause the child to think that the toy is bigger than it actually is. Speeded-up film may give the impression that the toy travels faster than it does, and using the sounds of a real motorcycle or racing car in the background may also give the child a false impression.

Given this information about the content of the commercials, the question that should be asked is: Do the commercials have any impact on children's and/or parents' behavior? The answer is a resounding *yes*. There is a significant amount of research evidence indicating that children are indeed influenced by the ads and then make specific requests of their parents, who then sometimes yield and purchase the products.

In a study entitled "Television and Social Behavior, Vol. IV. A Technical Report to the Surgeon General's Scientific Advisory Committee on Television and Social Behavior," mothers reported that toys were the second most frequently requested product, after breakfast cereals.

The age of the child was also a factor. Younger children, in the 5-to-7-year range, asked more frequently for the various products they saw advertised. Other studies have shown that younger children like the commercials better than the older children. They also did not know that the purpose of a commercial was to sell a product. It is interesting to note that while the older children asked for specific advertised products less frequently, they were more likely to get what they wanted. It may be that as the child becomes older, develops more fully his evaluative and critical skills, and learns to be more selective in his asking, the parent is more willing to take the request into consideration when making a purchase.

The more television the children watched, the more likely they were to ask for the advertised toys. Parents who watched more television themselves and tended to have more favorable attitudes toward television were more likely to yield to the requests for advertised toys. Now, armed with this research evidence, parents should be aware of the effects of television and toy advertising, and make some adjustments.

## Fighting Back

1. Don't depend totally on television advertising to dictate toy buying. If your child writes Santa a letter full of TV toys, have a conference and make suggestions or ask if there are other toys not on the list that he would like. You might want to yield and buy at least one of the strongly desired media toys so that you won't hear the plaintive cry on Christmas morning that "I didn't get what I asked for." You might also allow the child to choose his one TV-advertised toy himself.
2. Teach your child to be a discriminating commercial watcher. Point out some of the techniques—background sounds, speeded-up film, etc.—that may account for an unrealistic perception of how the toy will actually perform.
3. Tell your child (if he is old enough to understand) why you are rejecting the toy, whether it is because of the expense, poor play value, or other reasons.
4. As your child is probably paying more attention to the visual part of the commercial rather than the voice-over narration, repeat for him such auditory information as "requires assembly," "your parents put it together," "batteries required," and "parts sold separately."
5. Many of the toys that are advertised are the mechanical variety where the child sits by and watches the toy perform rather than *actively participating* in the play. This sort of passivity is anathema to the process of play. A few mechanical toys here and there will not have a devastating impact on the child; however, we should be aware that they do not promote active play. They are also likely to have complicated moving parts that are easily broken.
6. Many of the toys advertised on TV have tie-ins to media characters and personalities that really add nothing to their play value but seem to make them

highly desirable. A Johnny Bench batter-up toy, a pair of Superman roller skates, or a Strawberry Shortcake cosmetics kit feature popular names, but the characters these toys are identified with are not important to the use of the toy. It is another case altogether, of course, with such products as the Winnie the Pooh stuffed animal, or Muppets dolls and puppets—here the original characters that lend their images are integral to the appreciation and value of the toys.
7. You can always say *no* gently to television-advertised toys, explain why they are not desirable, and provide better alternatives for your child.

I don't want to leave the impression that all is negative on the part of television toy advertising. Recently we have seen some encouraging responses from manufacturers—ads for good solid toys of unlimited play value. A recent commercial for Playskool's Bristle Blocks showed a little girl playing with a construction toy. An ad for Milton Bradley's Memory Game promotes an inexpensive game that provides excellent opportunities for the development of concentration, memory, identification and matching abilities, and discerning spatial relationships. And Crayola crayon ads have emphasized the *active creativity* of the child. One can only hope that advertisements of this caliber and with this sort of focus are increasingly visible on the home screen in the future.

# 12
## Toy Safety

Before we get carried away by the glittering displays in the stores, let us keep a few sobering thoughts in mind as we choose toys. In 1979, according to estimates from the U.S. Consumer Product Safety Commission, more than 127,000 children under age 14 received hospital emergency room treatment for injuries related to toys. An estimated 503,600 people received injuries associated with bicycles; 65 percent of these injuries were sustained by children. Over 500,000 children under 14 years of age required treatment for skateboard-related injuries. These staggering figures, which do not include those injuries treated at home, serve to point out that choosing toys and supervising our children's play is a serious responsibility indeed. Knowing some of the dangers involved with toys and play will better prepare us all.

### Small Objects

Small objects that can be swallowed, inhaled, or lodged in the throat, ear, or nose are a major cause of injuries to children under the age of 5. Many of these objects—coins, jewelry, pins, needles, paper clips, tacks, screws, fishing equipment—were never intended for use by small children, who should not be given access to them. However, there are also many toys and parts of toys that can be dangerous if not properly selected and supervised.

No toy containing pieces less than one inch long or wide, or so small that they can be easily swallowed or embedded, should be bought for young children. These include such toys as mosaic tiles, marbles, beads, pegs, and small building components. Even if these toys are bought for older children, there is a possibility their younger siblings will get their hands on them, so parents must be aware of the dangers and supervise play accordingly.

Many injuries are caused by small parts of toys that have broken off. This points up the fact that we should inspect our children's toys often and repair or replace those that are damaged.

## *Swallowings or Ingestions*

Four-year-old Derek was playing tag with his older sister and a cousin. His sister discovered that he had a dime and a penny in his mouth. She tried to get them away from him but Derek ran away laughing. He stumbled and accidentally swallowed the coins. There was no pain in his throat or abdomen, and Derek's mother was told by the pediatrician just to watch his stools for the next few days to make sure the coins passed through his digestive system. They did pass through with no trouble.

Typically, ingestions of small round objects do not cause serious injury. Those that are harmful involve objects that become lodged in the throat or sharp objects, such as open safety pins, that cut the throat or other organs. Parents should always close safety pins before laying them down—a safety measure I learned from watching my pediatrician diaper my first child. If your child should swallow something like a tack, a piece of rigid plastic, or a needle, consult your doctor immediately or go at once to the nearest hospital emergency room.

One of the most life-threatening types of accidents are those involving objects that become lodged in the throat and obstruct breathing. In these cases it is vital to know how to do the Heimlich maneuver, which has become the standard emergency procedure. With the child's back to you, engage him in a bear hug. Make a fist, using both hands, right under the sternum (the center bone in the chest between the ribs), in the soft pit of the stomach. Remember to press against softness, not against bone. Then press in and upward in short, quick thrusts. Usually the object will be ejected from the throat.

The public library in your area might have a short film demonstrating the Heimlich maneuver; if so, it would be worthwhile to get a group of parents together to view it. You can also find posters explaining the technique displayed in many public eating places. It's a procedure everyone should know.

If an object is lodged in the throat that is *not* causing breathing difficulties, and you can see it, you might try to reach down into the throat and remove it. The Heimlich maneuver can also be used in these cases. If you cannot dislodge an object and it is obstructing breathing, call for an ambulance or rush the child to an emergency room, whichever is quicker.

## Inhalations

Two-year-old Denise crawled under the dining room table and found a small foam-rubber ball that belonged to her older sister. She began to chew off pieces of the ball. The mother discovered her eating the foam pieces and was able to get most of them from her. Two pieces, however, were inhaled into her left lung. She had to be hospitalized for surgical removal of the foam.

In the Consumer Product Safety Commission study previously mentioned, all of the children who inhaled objects into their tracheae (windpipes) or further into the bronchi or lungs required hospitalization. One victim died and, in other instances, portions of the lungs had to be removed. Thus we can see how important it is to supervise our children's play and make sure they do not put objects into their noses.

If a peanut is inhaled into the bronchus, a very serious condition called vegetal bronchitis can occur. Therefore, very young children of 3 and 4 years old should not be given peanuts to eat.

If your child does inhale a small object, call your pediatrician immediately or get your child to the nearest hospital emergency room as quickly as possible.

## Objects Lodged in the Nose or Ear

There is not as much *immediate* danger from something being lodged in the ear or nose, but the consequences can be very serious indeed. An object in the nose may be inhaled into the lungs, or begin to interfere with breathing. Objects lodged deeply in the ear canal can cause severe pain and/or ear infection, which may result in partial or complete hearing loss.

If there is something stuck in your child's nose, have him blow his nose, though not too forcibly. Don't ask a very young child to do this as he might inadvertently inhale the object further. You should not try to get the object out with tweezers or any similar object because this also increases the chance that it will be pushed further in. If the child cannot sneeze or blow the object out, call the doctor and/or go to the emergency room.

Sometimes objects can be stuck in a child's nose for several days before he will tell you about it or you will discover it. Changes in breathing patterns or a foul-smelling bloody discharge from one nostril are signs that this sort of problem might be present.

It is best not to try to get an object out of a child's ear yourself. Again, the safest thing to do is call your doctor.

## Projectiles

No toys involving projectiles should be allowed in the house when there are small children. These include darts, dart pistols, archery sets, and any other toy with parts that are propelled through the air with a great deal of force. They are hazardous and frequently cause injuries to the eyes. Even if a projectile toy is bought for an older child, he should be thoroughly instructed in its proper use and supervised when he plays with it.

### Electrical Toys

Toys that use electrical current in their operation pose special dangers. Not only do we parents have to watch for the usual hazards of sharp edges and movable parts that can inflict injury, but we must also be aware of the possibility of shocks and burns. Any electrical toy can potentially cause a shock. If the child touches one of the prongs of the plug while the other prong is making contact in the outlet, he will receive a shock. A toy that uses a light bulb, such as a play oven, will deliver a shock if the child sticks a finger in the empty socket while the toy is plugged in. In one instance, a little girl put one end of an electric cord that belonged in the transformer of a racing car into her mouth while the other end was plugged in. She was knocked unconscious by the shock, and if her older brother had not immediately summoned their mother, she might have died.

To protect children from some of the dangers inherent in electrical toys, the Consumer Product Safety Commission, under the Federal Hazardous Substances Act, issued safety regulations regarding their manufacture and performance. All electrical or moving parts that pose a specific hazard—the needle on a toy sewing machine, for example—must be enclosed in containers that the child will not be able to open. If the toy is to be used in or with water (not the best idea to begin with), the electrical components must be enclosed in a watertight, sealed container. Plugs should have a shield that flares out at the bottom to prevent the child from touching the electrically charged prong as he is plugging in or unplugging the toy. The plug should also be designed so that there are specific areas where it may be gripped by the finger and thumb. Some toys, such as the Fisher-Price Movie Viewer Theater, have a large box-shaped plug called a "toy transformer," with well-defined gripping areas. The underside bears a warning not to replace the toy transformer with a standard plug because an "electrical hazard may result."

Burns are another possible danger associated with electrical toys containing heating elements, such as toy ovens, irons, and woodburning kits. The Consumer Product Safety Commission has established regulations regarding safe temperature levels for the surfaces of these toys. The temperatures vary according to what surface it is: If there is a high probability that the child will touch the surface (for example, the outside of a toy oven), it cannot be very hot. The interior, which the child would normally not touch, is allowed to be a good bit hotter.

Heating elements are also required to be designed to protect the operator from shocks. Manufacturers cannot recommend any toy with a heating element for use by a child less than 8 years of age. Other toys that reach extremely high temperatures, such as woodburning kits, are suggested for use only by children 12 or older.

When we get ready to buy an electrical toy for our children, there are several important factors to consider. The first are the age and abilities of the child. Check the toy for the manufacturer's recommendations and use these as a guideline; remember, though, that these are the *minimum* suggested ages. Even though a toy stove may be recommended for children older than 8, there will undoubtedly be some 8-year-olds who are just not mature enough to own and operate it. Therefore, you should know the particular interests and abilities of the child you are buying for. A toy that is too complicated can invite misuse that will increase its hazards.

In fact, in his book *Toys That Don't Care*, Edward Swartz questions the value of buying electric toy appliances for children of any age. He argues that regular, full-sized appliances are sturdier and better designed and, therefore, safer in most instances. The child will tend not to think of a real appliance as a "harmless toy" and will probably treat it with more care.

It is best not to get electrical toys for children too young to plug them in. Thus it would be better to buy a battery-operated record player than an electrical one for a 3-year-old, even though the battery-operated machine may be less durable.

When the child is old enough to plug in an electrical device, show him how to do it correctly. He should grasp the plug by the designated thumb and finger areas. When he is removing it from the outlet, he should take hold of the plug itself, never the cord.

We can further reduce the hazards associated with electrical toys in several ways. Make sure that all electrical outlets not in use are covered with dummy plugs—plastic inserts that will keep children from sticking any foreign objects into the outlet. Before an electrical toy is played with, take the time to sit down with the child and read with him the instructions that accompany it. Keep the instruction booklet for future reference. *Demonstrate* the proper use of each toy to the child, and plan to supervise very carefully the first play activity with a new toy. Be aware of—and let the child know, too—the maintenance procedures necessary to keep electrical toys in good operating condition. They should be inspected frequently for signs of wear or breakage. And always keep in mind that electrical toys can be dangerous for young children even if they belong to their older brothers and sisters. Store them in a dry place toddlers cannot reach. In this as in many other aspects of child care, there is no substitute for parental supervision.

### *Rattles*

Rattles are typically one of the first toys given to an infant. Many times, the baby is too young to handle it properly and ends up reflexively striking himself in the head or face. Rattles and other hand-held toys should be introduced when, according to the baby's own particular growing pattern, he is able to reach for and grasp the toy voluntarily.

Very small rattles that fit inside the baby's mouth should be avoided. The Consumer Product Safety Commission reports that some infants have died as a result of swallowing or falling while sucking on a rattle, thereby jamming them down their throats. The types of rattles involved in these choking incidents were ones less than 1⅜-inch in diameter and shaped like telephone receivers, dumbbells, clothespins, and safety pins. The infant should be able to chew or suck on a rattle, but not insert it completely into the mouth. It is recommended that rattles be at least 3 inches in diameter.

They also should not be made of rigid plastic that can break and cause punctures or lacerations from the sharp edges. If any rattle is broken, it should be disposed of immediately. It's a wise practice to remove rattles and other small objects from the crib while the baby is sleeping.

## Balloons

Balloons are such commonly used toys that we may forget that in the wrong circumstances they can be deadly. In one report from the Consumer Product Safety Commission, balloons were found to be the cause of more deaths than any of the fourteen types of toys and products involved in the study. Parents or some other older person should blow up balloons for children until they are well past the age when they might accidentally inhale them. Children should never be allowed to chew on an uninflated balloon or the torn pieces of one that has burst. These may be accidentally swallowed and block the air passage. Even though balloons are a lot of fun, they cannot be considered totally harmless, and caution should be exercised when they are given to young children.

## Bicycles

Bicycles account for almost a half-million injuries per year, and a significant percentage of those injuries involve children. This is not to say that you should not buy a bicycle for your child, but it does mean that particular care should be taken in selecting and maintaining the bike, as well as teaching your child to ride it.

If at all possible, buy a bike that meets the Consumer Product Safety Commission standards. The bicycle should be labeled accordingly if it does meet these standards. To be certain, ask the salesperson.

Choose the proper-sized bike for your child. Buying one that the child will "grow into" may be economically sensible, but there is an increased risk of injury because the child may not be able to adequately control it.

When buying a boy's bike, the child should be able to straddle the middle bar with both feet on the ground. There should be about an inch of space between the bar and the inseam of the child's pants. As for a girl's bike, the child should be able to sit on the seat, and with the leg fully extended, reach the pedal's lowest position. As the child grows, the seat and handlebars can be adjusted to accommodate.

Handlebars can be either the standard, curved type (such as those found on three- and ten-speed bikes), or the high-rise type. The standard handlebars and the upper part of the curved handlebars should be the same level as the seat. The high-rise handlebars should be lower than the rider's shoulder. The high-rise types do not allow for the more natural bending of the arms that you get with the standards, and they can make balancing on the bike more awkward, but they seem to be a particular status symbol in the pre-ten-speed set.

If your child is just moving up to a two-wheeler from a tricycle or one of the Big Wheel vehicles, it is probably best to put training wheels on until the child has gotten used to it. Make sure that the training wheels are installed properly: When the bike is balanced on two wheels, both training wheels will be off the ground. It is only if the child leans to one side or the other that the training wheels come into use, giving an added measure of stability. When you see that the training wheels are consistently staying off the ground, your child is maintaining his balance and can probably manage without them.

The bicycle should be cared for and kept in good working condition. It should never be left outside overnight. Check it periodically for damaged or missing parts, such as lost handgrips or pedals, loose seats, or defective brakes.

Sometimes bicycle maintenance workshops for children are sponsored by recreation agencies. This would be particularly valuable for your child as he or she graduates to a ten-speed bike. If there is no workshop available, a group of parents in conjunction with some bicycle merchants might sponsor one for interested children and adults.

Many times the injuries sustained by bicycle riders are not due to the bicycle, but to the actions of the rider. Children should be thoroughly instructed about safe bicycle-riding practices. They should never ride two on a bike—this makes it unstable. There is also a chance that the second rider will catch his feet in the spokes. The rider should obey all traffic signals. He should maintain a safe speed—one that allows him to be in control of the bike at all times. Stunts should be left to the professionals—though everybody will try to accomplish the feat of riding with no hands. (When this came up with my children, I casually acknowledged it, but did not praise them or make an issue out of it because I did not want to inspire them to try greater stunts.)

Teach your child to avoid sudden braking as this can sometimes cause accidents. If a dog chases him while he is on his bike, it is probably best not to try to outride or outwit the animal. He should jump off the bike on the side opposite the dog, using his bike as a shield to protect him from it, and scream for help.

## *Tricycles*

Tricycles also cause a significant number of injuries to children. If you buy a metal tricycle rather than a Big Wheel, be sure that the tricycle is the right size for the child. If his feet can barely reach the pedals, he cannot control it. As with bicycles, children should be cautioned not to ride "double" because this increases the chances of the tricycle tipping over. It's hard to understand why manufacturers still design tricycles with that "perfect place" on the back for another child to stand.

Since tricycles have no brakes, going down a hill can be very dangerous. A tricycle can pick up a tremendous amount of speed and, if the child's feet cannot touch the ground, there is no way to stop it. The child should also be warned to keep hands and feet away from the tricycle's moving spokes. Tricycles should not be left outdoors, as moisture can cause the metal parts to rust.

It would seem that a Big or Little Wheel toy, even though it is made of plastic and doesn't last as long as a metal tricycle, is a safer choice for several reasons. The wide-spaced wheels and close-to-the-ground, low-slung seats offer greater stability and reduce the chances of the vehicle turning over, even on fast turns. If the child does fall, it is from a lower height than he would from a metal tricycle. Also, with the Big Wheel, there are no spokes in which the child's hands or feet may be caught. Since the construction is primarily plastic, there is no chance of rust weakening the vehicle and less chance of injury from sharp edges or points. Finally, because the child is closer to the ground, he is better able to use his feet as a brake. Of course this is not the most desirable treatment for shoes, but sometimes you have to give a little to get a little.

One very real danger that exists with the Big Wheel, however—just as it does with the tricycle—is the level of speed that can be reached traveling down an incline. Because the Big Wheel is so low, if the child rolls into the street, especially between parked cars, a motorist might not see him until it is too late. If there is an incline in the child's play area, he is going to roll down it, and it does little good to tell him not to—that's where the fun is. Thus we must make our children fully aware of the dangers of riding into the street, especially in busy traffic areas. They should be shown how to turn just before they get to the bottom of a hill. And they should be supervised as closely as possible until it is clear that they understand and follow the best practices.

## Skateboards

Skateboarding requires a very complex coordination of sensory, perceptual, and motor skills, more so than almost any other common sports activity. The skateboarder must evaluate a constant stream of information about the terrain and other aspects of the environment, and use this information to make split-second motor and muscular responses in order to navigate and control the board. Any false movement may cause the rider to lose his balance, fall, and sustain a serious injury.

It can conservatively be said that *no child under 5 years of age* possesses the muscular control and skills of balance necessary to use a skateboard safely. A child that age is also unable to take in and process all of the necessary visual and auditory information. Thus we should not even consider a skateboard for the preschool child.

The safest place to use a skateboard is a smooth-paved area with no automobile traffic. Irregularities in the riding surface, such as cracks, holes, dips, bumps, or rocks lying around, cause accidents. This kind of perfection, of course, is hard to find. Certainly children should avoid heavily trafficked areas. I have seen youngsters skating downtown in the midst of rush-hour traffic. This practice should be prohibited.

Skateboard injuries are often very severe. The most common is a fracture to the lower arm or lower leg. However, injuries involving joints, internal organs, and the head do often occur. Protective equipment such as helmets, wrist braces, and knee and arm padding can help safeguard the rider, though they provide no guarantee. Children should be taught how to fall so that the fall is broken with the hands, and there is less possibility of injury to the back or head. This is easier to do if they fall forward or to the side.

Most skateboard injuries are caused by a flaw in the riding

surface, by a collision with a car or other obstacle, or by the rider's losing balance or making an incorrect muscular response. Usually the skateboard itself is not at fault, although there have been some consumer complaints of wheels coming off or boards cracking. Skateboarding is a complex skill, one that should be learned slowly and undertaken with a great deal of care and common sense.

# Bibliography

Adler, Richard, et al. *The Effects of Television Advertising on Children: Review and Recommendations.* Lexington, Mass.: D. C. Heath and Co., 1980.

Arbuthnot, May Hill, and Sutherland, Zena. *Children and Books.* Glenview, Ill.: Scott, Foresman and Co., 1972.

Ariès, Philippe. *Centuries of Childhood: A Social History of Family Life.* Translated by Robert Baldick. New York: Alfred A. Knopf, 1962.

Barcus, F. Earle. *Children's Television: An Analysis of Programming and Advertising.* New York: Praeger Publishers, 1977.

Barry, Thomas E. *Children's Television Advertising.* Chicago: American Marketing Association, 1978.

Bjorklund, Gail. *Planning for Play: A Developmental Approach.* Columbus, Ohio: Charles E. Merrill Publishing Co., 1978.

Canadian Toy Testing Council. *The Toy Report: A Buyer's Guide to Toys.* Ottawa, Ontario: Tyrell Press, 1981.

Clark, Barbara. *Growing Up Gifted: Developing the Potential of Children at Home and at School.* Columbus, Ohio: Charles E. Merrill Publishing Co., 1979.

Ellenburg, M. Kelly. *Effanbee: The Dolls with the Golden Hearts.* North Kansas City, Mo.: Trojan Press, 1973.

Ellis, Michael J. *Why People Play.* Englewood, N.J.: Prentice-Hall, 1973.

Foley, Dan. *Toys through the Ages.* Philadelphia: Chilton Books, 1962.

Hartley, Ruth E.; Frank, Lawrence K.; and Goldenson, Robert M. *Understanding Children's Play.* New York: Columbia University Press, 1969.

Hegeler, Sten. *Choosing Toys for Children.* London: Tavistock Publications, 1963.

Hils, Karl. *The Toy: Its Value, Construction and Use*. Chester, Penn.: Dufor Editions, 1961.

Jacobs, Flora Gill. *A History of Doll Houses*. New York: Charles Scribner's Sons, 1953.

Kastein, Shulamith; Spaudling, Isabelle; and Scharf, Battia. *Raising the Young Blind Child: A Guide for Parents and Educators*. New York: Human Sciences Press, 1980.

Kaye, Evelyn. *The Family Guide to Children's Television: What to Watch, What to Miss, What to Change and How to Do It*. New York: Pantheon Books, 1974.

Kaye, Marvin. *A Toy Is Born*. New York: Stein and Day, 1973.

King, Constance Eileen. *The Encyclopedia of Toys*. New York: Crown Publishers, 1978.

Melody, William. *Children's TV: The Economics of Exploitation*. New Haven: Yale University Press, 1973.

Millar, Susanna. *The Psychology of Play*. Baltimore: Penguin Books, 1968.

Page, Hilary F. *Playtime in the First Five Years*. Philadelphia: J. B. Lippincott Co., 1954.

Rees, Elizabeth Lodge, Dr. *A Doctor Looks at Toys*. Springfield, Ill.: Charles C. Thomas, 1961.

Rubinstein, Eli; Comstock, George A.; and Murray, John P., eds. *Television in Day-to-Day Life—Patterns of Use: A Technical Report to the Surgeon General's Scientific Advisory Committee on Television and Social Behavior*. Television and Social Behavior Reports and Papers, vol. 4. Washington, D.C.: U.S. Govt. Printing Office.

St. George, Eleanor. *The Dolls of Yesterday*. New York: Charles Scribner's Sons, 1948.

Schwartz, Marvin. *F.A.O. Schwarz through the Years*. New York: Doubleday and Co., 1975.

Schofield, Angela. *Toys in History*. East Sussex, England: Wayland Publishing, 1978.

Swartz, Edward. *Toys That Don't Care*. Boston: Gambit, 1971.

Tilney, Phillip. *Play's the Thing*. Canada: National Museums, 1978.

Tudor-Hart, Beatrix. *Toys Play and Discipline*. London: Routledge and Kegan Paul, 1955.

See also pages 43–44 for some suggestions for further reading on art activities for children, page 152 for books discussing children with disabilities, and pages 163–165 for books on creating homemade toys.

# Directory of Sources and Manufacturers

Adica Pongo
2 Victor St.
Lodi, N.J. 07644

Aero Educational Products Ltd.
P.O. Box 71
St. Charles, Ill. 60174

Alexander Doll Company
615 W. 131 St.
New York, N.Y., 10027

American Art Clay
4717 W. 16th St.
Indianapolis, Ind. 46222

American Crayon Co.
1706 Hayes Ave.
Sandusky, Ohio 44870

American Toy and Furniture Company
5933 N. Lincoln Ave.
Chicago, Ill. 60659

AMF Voit Inc.
3801 S. Harbor Blvd.
Santa Ana, Calif. 92704

AMF Wheel Goods
P.O. Box 344
Olney, Ill. 62450

Animal Fair, Inc.
P.O. Box 189
Chanhassen, Maine 55317

Art Chemical Products, Inc.
1019 Salamonie Ave.
Huntington, Ind. 46750

Associated Hobby Manufacturers
401 E. Tioga St.
Philadelphia, Pa. 19134

Atari, Inc.
Consumer Division
1195 Barregas Ave.
Sunnyvale, Ca. 94086

Atlanta Novelty Company
1911 Park Ave.
New York, N.Y. 10035

The Avalon Hill Game Co.
4517 Hartford Rd.
Baltimore, Md. 21214

Avalon Industries
95 Lorimer St.
Brooklyn, N.Y. 11206

Ava International
P.O. Box 7611
Waco, Tex. 76710

## DIRECTORY OF SOURCES AND MANUFACTURERS

Breyer Molding Company
222 N. Maplewood Ave.
Chicago, Ill. 60612

Brio Scanditoy Corporation
6531 North Sidney Place
Milwaukee, Wis. 53209

Buddy L.
Henry Katz Organization
200 Fifth Ave.
New York, N.Y. 10010

Cadaco
310 W. Polk St.
Chicago, Ill. 60607

California Stuffed Toys
611 S. Anderson St.
Los Angeles, Calif. 90023

Caran D'Ache of Switzerland
454 Third Ave.
New York, N.Y. 10016

Chemtoy Corporation
4700 W. 19th St.
Cicero, Ill. 60650

Childcraft Education Corporation
20 Kolmer Rd.
Edison Township, N.J. 08817

Child Guidance. *See* Gabriel Industries

Coleco Industries
945 Asylum Ave.
Hartford, Conn. 06105

Colorforms
Walnut St.
Norwood, N.J. 07648

Dakin and Company
P.O. Box 7746
Rincon Annex
San Francisco, Calif. 94120

DeKalb Toys Inc.
11 and Oak St.
P.O. Box 157
DeKalb, Ill. 60115

Dennison Manufacturing Company
300 Howard St.
Framingham, Mass. 01701

Design R. Crafts
3030 W. Pafford St.
Fort Worth, Tex. 76110

Dolly Toy Company
320 North Fourth St.
Tipp City, Ohio 45371

Duplo. *See* Lego Systems

Eastern Doll Corporation
37–43 Greene St.
New York, N.Y. 10013

Eden Toys
112 W. 13th St.
New York, N.Y. 10011

Edu-Cards
Div. of Binney-Smith, Inc.
1100 Church Lane
P.O. Box 431
Easton, Pa. 18042

Effanbee Doll Corporation
200 Fifth Ave.
New York, N.Y. 10010

Elka Toys
200 Fifth Ave., Suite 524
New York, N.Y. 10010

Ellanee Doll Company
505 Driggs Ave.
Brooklyn, N.Y. 11211

Empire of Carolina
Div. of Carolina Enterprises, Inc.
41 Madison Ave., 27th floor
New York, N.Y. 10010

Entex Industries, Inc.
100 W. Walnut St.
Compton, Calif.

Epoch Playthings
200 Fifth Ave.
New York, N.Y. 10010

## DIRECTORY OF SOURCES AND MANUFACTURERS

Eugene Doll and Novelty Company
200 Fifth Ave.
New York, N.Y. 10010

E. E. Fairchild Corporation
82 East Main St.
Webster, N.Y. 14580

Fisher-Price Toys
636 Girard Ave.
East Aurora, N.Y. 14052

Gabriel Industries
41 Madison Ave.
New York, N.Y. 10010

GAF Corporation
140 W. 51st St.
New York, N.Y. 10020

Ganz Bros. Toys Ltd.
39 Orfus Rd.
Toronto, Ontario M6A IL7

Gayla Industries
6401 Antoine St.
Houston, Tex. 77018

Genie Toys, Inc.
2200 Lucas Ave.
St. Louis, Mo. 63103

Gym-Dandy Inc.
200 Fifth Ave.
New York, N.Y. 10010

Hasbro
1027 Newport Ave.
Pawtucket, R.I. 02861

Hedstrom Company
Sunnyside Rd.
Bedford, Pa. 15522

HiFlyer Manufacturing Co.
510 E. Wabash Ave.
Decatur, Ill. 62525

Hobbies International
P.O. Box 1121
Tustin, Calif. 92680

Hohner, Inc.
Andrews Rd.
Hicksville, N.Y. 11802

Horsman Dolls, Inc.
200 Fifth Ave., Suite 1440
New York, N.Y. 10010

House of Games
2633 Greenleaf Ave.
Elk Grove Village, Ill. 60007

Ideal Toy Corporation
184-10 Jamaica Ave.
Hollis, N.Y. 11423

Illfelder Toy Co.
915 Broadway
New York, N.Y. 10010

Imperial Crayon Company
649 Lexington Ave.
Brooklyn, N.Y. 11221

International Games
457 N. Ottawa
Joliet, Ill. 60435

Invicta Plastics
200 Fifth Ave., Suite 940
New York, N.Y. 10010

Jak-Pak Inc.
P.O. Box 374
Milwaukee, Wis. 53201

Jaymar Specialty
219 36th St.
Brooklyn, N.Y. 11232

Jester Toys International Ltd.
5 Lucon Drive
Deer Park, N.Y. 11729

Jewel Leather Goods Co.
154 Grand St.
New York, N.Y. 10013

Johnson & Johnson Baby Products Co.
220 Centennial Ave.
Piscataway, N.J. 08854

Kenner Products Co.
1014 Vine St.
Cincinnati, Ohio 45202

Knickerbocker Toys
1107 Broadway
New York, N.Y. 10010

Kohner, Inc.
Subs. of Gabriel Industries
200 Fifth Ave.
New York, N.Y. 10010

Lakeside Industries
4400 W. 78th St.
Minneapolis, Minn. 55435

Lebanon Ball Co.
11th Ave. and E. Cumberland St.
Lebanon, Pa. 17042

Lego Systems, Inc.
555 Taylor Rd.
Enfield, Conn. 06082

Little Tikes, Inc.
8705 Freeway Dr.
Macedonia, Ohio 44056

LJN Toys, Inc.
200 Fifth Ave.
New York, N.Y. 10010

Lowe
Samuel Lowe Co.
1324 52nd St.
Kenosha, Wis. 53140

Magic Marker Corporation
Cherry Hill Industrial Park
Cherry Hill, N.J. 08003

Marvel Toy Co.
226-34 77th Ave.
Bayside, N.Y. 11364

Marx Toys
45 Church St.
Stamford, Conn. 06904

Mattel Toys
5150 Rosecrans Ave.
Hawthorn, Calif. 90250

Mego Corporation
41 Madison Ave.
New York, N.Y. 10010

Mighty Star Ltd.
200 Fifth Ave.
New York, N.Y. 10010

Milton Bradley Company
Shaker and Denslow Rds.
East Longmeadow, Mass. 01108

Mirro Aluminum Co.
1512 Washington St.
Manitowoc, Wis. 54220

Modern Crafts Co.
6333 Etzel Ave.
St. Louis, Mo. 63133

Monogram Models Inc.
8601 Waukegan Rd.
Morton Grove, Ill. 60053

[Peggy] Nisbet Ltd.
Oldmixon Crescent
Weston-Super-Mare
Avon, England BS24 9ED 21141

Nylint Corporation
1800 16th St.
Rockford, Ill. 61101

Ohio Art Co.
P.O. Box 111
Bryan, Ohio 43508

Parker Brothers
190 Bridge St.
Salem, Mass. 01970

Playjour. *See* GAF

Playskool Inc.
4501 W. Augusta Blvd.
Chicago, Ill. 60651

Pressman Toy Corp.
200 Fifth Ave.
New York, N.Y. 10010

Questor Education Products
1055 Bronx River Ave.
Bronx, N.Y. 10472

# DIRECTORY OF SOURCES AND MANUFACTURERS

Rapco
500 N. Spaulding Ave.
Chicago, Ill. 60624

Replica Models Inc.
800 Slaters Lane
Alexandria, Va. 22314

Revell Inc.
4223 Glencoe
Venice, Calif. 90291

Roller Derby Skate Corporation
311 W. Edwards St.
Litchfield, Ill. 62056

Rushton Company
1275 Ellsworth Drive N.W.
Atlanta, Ga. 30325

Sargent Art Inc.
100 E. Diamond Ave.
Hazelton, Pa. 18201

Schaper Manufacturing Co.
9909 South Shore Drive
Minneapolis, Minn. 55441

Schwinn Bicycle Co.
1856 N. Kostner Ave.
Chicago, Ill. 60639

Scientific Models Inc.
340 Snyder Ave.
Verkeley Heights, N.J. 07992

Selchow & Righter Co.
2215 Union Blvd.
Bay Shore, N.Y. 11706

Shindana Toys
6107 S. Central Ave.
Los Angeles, Calif. 90001

Skaneateles Handicrafters Inc.
Skanaeteles, N.Y. 13152

Sommer Metalcraft Corporation
315 Poston Drive
Crawfordsville, Ind. 47933

[Margarete] Steiff Inc.
GmbH Alleenstr. D-7928
Glengen/Brenz, Germany

Superior Toy and Manufacturing Co.
3417 N. Halstead
Chicago, Ill. 60657

Tasco Sales Inc.
1075 N.W. 71st St.
Miami, Fla. 33138

Texas Instruments
P.O. Box 53
Lubbock, Tex. 79408

Textors Corporation
620 Buckbee St.
Rockford, Ill. 61101

Tomy
901 E. 233 St.
Carson, Calif. 90745

Tonka Toys
5300 Shoreline Blvd.
Mond, Minn. 55364

Tootsietoy Division Strombecker Corp.
600 N. Pulaski Rd.
Chicago, Ill. 60624

TSR (Dungeons and Dragons)
TSR Hobbies, Inc.
P.O.B. 756
Lake Geneva, Wis. 53147

Tudor Games, Inc.
176 Johnson St.
Brooklyn, N.Y. 11201

Uncle Milton Ant Farms
10459 N. Jefferson Blvd.
Culver City, Calif. 90230

Uneeda Doll Co.
200 Fifth Ave.
New York, N.Y. 10010

Uniroyal Inc.
1230 Avenue of the Americas
New York, N.Y. 10020

U.S. Games Corporation
2908 Corvin Drive
Santa Clara, Calif. 95051

Utility Chemical Company
Sixth Ave. and Wall St.
Paterson, N.J. 07542

Vanity Fair Industries
260 Bethpage-Spagnoli Rd.
Melville, N.Y. 11746

Vogue Dolls Inc.
184 Commercial St.
Malden, Mass. 02148

Walco Products
1200 Zerega Ave.
Bronx, N.Y. 10462

Western Publishing Co.
1220 Mound Ave.
Racine, Wis. 53403

Western Toy Manufacturing Co.
3833 S.E. Milwaukee Ave.
Portland, Oreg. 97202

Whitehall Games Inc.
5 Bridge St.
Watertown, Mass. 02172

Wonder Products Co.
151 S. Main St.
Collierville, Tenn. 38017

# Index

*Note:* Numbers in *italics* refer to illustrations.

Action for Children's Television, 167–69
action toys, 31, 38
adult participation, 7–9
alphabet blocks, 28
alphabet books, 106–7
alphabet tiles, home-made, 162–63
animals, stuffed, 69–73
   for infants, 71
   literary characters, 72
   realistic, 71–72
anxiety play, 34–35
assembling toys, 28
auditory stimulation, 19–20

baby dolls, 61–62
balloons, danger from, 179
Barcus, F. Earle, 167–69
bath toys, 23
bean bags, home-made, 160
Bettelheim, Bruno, 129–30
bicycles, danger from, 179–81
blind children, 138–51
   animal toys, 142
   artistic development, 149
   books for, 146–47
   electronic toys, 149–51
   manual dexterity, 143–44
   musical toys, 145–46
   physical development, 144–45
   recognition skills, 147–48
   spelling, 150
   tub toys, 141
   vocabulary, 142
blocks, 6, 34, 46
books
   abecedarium, 106
   animal tales, 119–20
   anxiety problems, 120–22
   artwork, 118–19
   bedtime, 121
   biographies, 125
   Caldecott, 115–18
   cause-and-effect, 140–41
   counting, 106
   fairy tales, 129–30
   first, 29–30, 105–12
   folktales, 123
   for gifted children, 138
   historical fiction, 124–25
   home-made, 159

books *(continued)*
  independent reading, 123–24
  late childhood, 124
  library, 111–12
  "Mother Goose," 108–10
  musical toys, 138–40
  Newbery Medal winners, 127–29
  picture, 113–14
  reading list, 130–32
  about school, 121
  on separation, 121–22
  on sibling rivalry, 122
  storybooks, 119–24
  subtlety in, 122–23
boxes, toy, 12
building toys, 28
buying toys, 31, 33

Caldecott books, 115–18
cause and effect, 22–24
*Children's Television: The Economics of Exploitation* (Melody), 166–67
clay, 41–42
cleaning up, 13
cognitive development, 34
concentration, 4
construction toys, 28, 34, 44–46, 45, 52
  for blind children, 142–43
constructive activities, 136–37
Consumer Product Safety Commission, 176
control, over environment, 53
coordination, 6, 28
costumes, 5
crayons, 29, 41
creative activities, 34
  games, 136–37
Creative Parenting Institute, 144, 149
creative play, 38–48
creative projects, books about, 43–44
creative toys, *42*, 43
creativity, 29, 41
crib gym, 22

crib toys, 21, 24

danger
  avoiding
    burns, 177
    electrical objects, 176–77
    inhalations, 174–75
    projectiles, 175–76
    swallowing, 173–74
  from toys
    balloons, 179
    bicycles, 179–81
    rattles, 178–79
    skateboards, 183–84
    tricycles, 181–83
deaf children, 151
deduction games, 102
disabled children, 151–52
discovery, 49
dollhouses, 35, 74–82
  American, 78–79
  for boys, 81–82
  choosing, 79–82
  decorating, 81
  Dutch, 76–77
  English, 77–78
  French, 77
  German, 76
  history, 74–79
dolls, 20, 35, 60–69
  baby, *65*
  Barbie, 66–67
  for boys, 63–64
  "cause and effect," 62
  choosing, 68–69
  collectors', 65
  in early childhood, 64–66
  fashion, *65*, 66
  history of, 60–62
  for infants, 62–63
  in late childhood, 66–67
  mechanical, 67–68, 69
  rag, 20, 62
  realistic, 63–64
  vinyl, 63
  talking, 62
  walking, 62
drawing, 39–41

electronic toys, 98, *99*
environment, varying, 17–19
experimentation, 4–5, 26, 33, 137
exploration, 137
  toys, 56, *57*, 58
externality, 23

fairy tales, 129–30
fantasy play, 4, 34, 35–36
fears, subconscious, 4
Federal Hazardous Substances Act, 176–77
finger development, 46
finger muscles, 85
Fraser, Antonia, 99–100

games, 87–100
  accumulation, 95–96
  balance, 97–98
  best buys, 103
  card, 94–95
  configuration, 92–93
  coordination, 97–98
  deduction, 96, 101, 102
  educational, 102–4
  electronic, 98–100
  eye–hand coordination, 97
  horoscope, 101
  informational, 96–97
  logic, 96
  memory, 101, 102
  positional, 92–93
    for preschoolers, 89–90
    quiz, 96–97
    race, 91–92
    for school-age children, 90
    sensory-motor coordination, 84
    skills acquisition, 87–88
    sports, 100–101
    strategy, 101, 102
    target, 101
    time element, 97
    video, 103–4
    war, 94
    wood, 93–94
gifted children, 133–38, *136*
  books for, 137–38
  toys and games for, 135–37

Halloween, 4
hearing, sense of, 16
*History of Toys, A* (Fraser), 99–100
hobbies, 59
home-made toys, 159–63
  books on, 163–65
hospital play, 25, *36*

illness, 152–58
  hospital games, 157–58
  toys during
    board games, 156–57
    construction toys, 154–55
    creative toys, 154
    dramatic play toys, 155
    exploration toys, 155–56
    musical, 155
imagination, 35
infancy, 21–23
  play during, 2–3
intellect, and play, 3–4
intellectual development, 26, 33
  toys for, 48–52
internal-external control, 22–23
internality, 23

Jack-in the-box, 23
James, William, 14–15

language, 33
learning, 14–15
*Lively Art of Picture Books, The* (Sendak), 8

magic markers, 29
mathematical toys, 58–59
  games, 102
Melody, William, 166
memory games, 102
*Miniature Collector*, 79
mirrors, nonbreakable, 21
mobiles, 19
"Mother Goose," 107, 108–110
mouth stimulation, 20
muscle coordination, 14
musical sounds, 34
musical toys, 19, 23, 46–48

National Library Service for the Blind and Physically Handicapped, 147
nesting toys, 26–28, *51*
Newbery Medal books, 127–29
noise toys, 23, 24
number blocks, 28
nursery rhymes, 30, 46, 107–10
nursery toys, 18–19
*Nutshell News*, 79, 81

Office of the Gifted and Talented, 133

pajamas, 18
paper dolls, 37
physical development, 5–7, 25–26, 33
  toys for, 52–56
physical skills, 53–54
play
  associative, 3–5
  complexity, 4
  concept of, 1–2
  solitary, 3
playhouse, 38
playmates, imaginary, 35, 37
playpen toys, 21
play space, 11–12
power, 40
pretending, 34
push-and-pull toys, 23, 25, 54
puzzles, 4, 83–87, *86*
  age groups, 86
  attention span, 85
  blind children, 143–44
  choosing, 85–87
  concentration, 85
  for gifted children, 135
  home-made, 160–61
  problem-solving skills, 85
  sensory-motor coordination, 84
  spatial relationships, 85
  wooden, 85

rattles, 14, 24–25
  danger from, 178–79
reading
  encouraging, 112–13
  to infant, 106
reversibility, 28, 50–51
ride-on toys, 25–26, *55*

safety. *See* danger; dangerous toys
self-awareness, 21–24
Sendak, Maurice, 8
shape perception, 26
skateboards, 183–84
singing, 46
smell, sense of, 15–16
social skills, 6–7
sounds, 19–20
spatial relationships, 26
spelling games, 102
squeeze toys, 23
stacking toys, 26–28
storage, 12–13
strategy toys, 102
sucking, 20
Swartz, Edward, 177
symbolic play, 4, 32, 33–48

taste, 16
teaching toys, 48–52
Teddy Bears, 70–71
teething, 20, 21, 23
telephone, 25
television
  commercials, 166–71
  counteracting negative effects, 170–71
theater toys, 48
touch, 16
*Toys That Don't Care* (Swartz), 177
tub toys, 21

U.S. Consumer Product Safety Commission, 172, 179
*Uses of Enchantment, The* (Bettelheim), 129–30

vehicles, 38
verbal symbols, 33
vision, 16–17
visual scanning, 85
voice development, 46

FUNDERBURG LIBRARY

MANCHESTER COLLEGE